W9-CKF-098

Bed and Breakfast
GUIDE
• • • • • • • • • • • • • • • FOR • • • • • • • • • • • • • • •
FOOD LOVERS

DEDICATED TO
Lesli Romero, my
compassion.com
child, and
Airman Clara Valdes

& THANKS
Senior Editor
Laurence Blanchette
—Brava!
Culinary editors
Chloe Frederickson,
Suzanne Beneit,
Katrina Bergstrom,
Christina Wilson,
Janet Jenkins,
Pamela Balyeat,
Julie Kimball and
Brian McKim
And a very special
thank you to designer
Laura Lamar and
our friends at the-
Culinary Institute of
America, Napa,
and the Santa Rosa
Junior College
Culinary Program.
Special thanks to all
of the team at
Bed & Breakfast Inns
and Guesthouses
International,
especially member-
ship director
Shannon Holl, and
Justina Long-Am,
Nicole Day,
Gini Rhoda,
Amber Janke, and
Steve Kelez.

Innkeeping is both a
lifestyle and an
avocation—innkeep-
ers are in the front-
lines of providing
hospitality, comfort,
and succor to weary
travelers—well done!

The information in this book was supplied in large part by the inns themselves, and is subject to change without notice. We strongly recommend that you call ahead to verify the information presented here before making final plans or reservations. The author and publisher make no representation that this book is accurate or complete. Errors and omissions, whether typographical, clerical, or otherwise, may sometimes occur herein.

The information about the properties in this publication is intended for personal use only. Any and all commercial use of the information in this publication is strictly prohibited.

This book may not be reproduced in whole or in part in any form or by any means, electronic or mechanical, including photocopying, recording, or by any informtion storage and retrieval system now known or hereafter invented, without written permission from the publisher.

The images in this book are representive of the B&B lifestyle and cuisine, and do not exactly reflect the recipes in this book.

© 2010 by Lanier Publishing International, Ltd.
All rights reserved.
Published 2010.
ISBN 978-0-9843766-6-7

This book can be ordered by mail from the publisher. Please include $3.50 for postage and handling for each copy. But try your local bookstore first!

Lanier Publishing International, Ltd.

PO Box 2240
Petaluma, CA 94953
tel. 707.763.0271
fax. 707.763.5762
e-mail lanier@travelguides.com

Find us on the internet at:
www.LanierBB.com
www.TravelGuideS.com

Distributed to the book trade by:
National Book Network
15200 NBN Way, Bldg. B
Blue Ridge Summit, PA 21264-2188
website: nbnbooks.com
tel. 1-800-462-6420

Design & Illustrations by MAX DESIGN STUDIO.*net*

Bed and Breakfast
GUIDE
•••••••••••••••• FOR ••••••••••••••••
FOOD LOVERS

Over 130 Choice Recipes for
Morning, Noon and Night from the Kitchens of
Inns and B&B's in All Fifty States

Bed and Breakfast Collection™

BY PAMELA LANIER

LANIER PUBLISHING INTERNATIONAL, LTD.
Petaluma, California

Contents

Contents

Contents

Introduction

Nothing says hospitality quite like a scrumptious home-cooked meal. These innkeeper-proven winners are a delight.

BED AND BREAKFAST (B&B) INNS allow the traveler to be immersed in the elegance of an Antebellum plantation, to sleep in an historic landmark, to get away from it all on a Colorado ranch, or to experience life in a Victorian mansion. Whatever the setting, the personal and convivial atmosphere of a B&B provides the chance to make new friends and relax while vacationing. All the little B&B extras that one doesn't expect from an impersonal hotel add up to a special travel experience that is winning the hearts of all who travel the B&B route.

Of course, FOOD is an essential ingredient in the B&B experience. This cookbook is a collection of innkeepers' favorite recipes of outstanding regional American cuisine, from *New Orleans-style BBQ Shrimp*, to *Maine Blueberry Pancakes*, to Southwestern *Huevos Rancheros* and *Blue Corn Waffles*.

Just like the rest of us, innkeepers come up short on time, too. That's why we've included a few recipes spread throughout, of inn-themed delights made with that all-American icon since 1930, "JIFFY" Mix. Even my Aunt Tommie, innkeeper and Southern cook extraordinaire, kept a few boxes of "JIFFY" Corn Muffin Mix stashed in her pantry for just those times when it was a corn muffin emergency—"JIFFY" Mix to the rescue. My Aunt Carrie's Hungarian Coffee Cake is a wonderful recipe, but time-consuming, so I adapted it to use "JIFFY" Baking Mix, and, voilá! Half the time or less—and no one has spotted the difference. Inspired by my daughter Clara, who is a corn dog fan, I developed the *Hot Diggity Dog Corn Muffins*, which have become a huge hit at our house. You can let your young guest help mix the batter while you cut up the hot dogs, and 15 minutes later, serve a scrumptious treat sure to put a smile on their faces.

*M*ost of these recipes are simple and easy to prepare, but they cover a wide range of cooking styles from a diverse variety of kitchens. To make the preparation of the dishes easier, we have endeavored to standardize the measurements and procedures—without distracting from the unique style of each contributing chef. When you visit each inn, you can taste its specialties for yourself.

Please tell them Pamela Lanier sent you!

BON APPÉTIT!

Breakfast
and Brunch

AMERICAN BED AND BREAKFASTS are cele-
brated around the world for their unforgettable
morning meals. With a winning combination of
fresh ingredients and a creative mind, innkeepers
across the country have delighted their guests
with breakfast dishes ranging from traditional
French Toast to elaborate egg dishes. In the
following pages, you'll find dozens of guest-
approved breakfast recipes sure to enchant your
family and friends right in your own kitchen.
This too-often-rushed meal can be transformed
into a delightfully lazy affair. And make-ahead
dishes like homemade granola or night-before
breakfast casseroles will help you enjoy a tasty
breakfast even on the most hectic mornings.

Brunch is a felicitous combination of breakfast and lunch that should be savored in pleasant
surroundings with good company. So gather
your loved ones together, and prepare some of
these time-tested recipes from inns across
America. Choose from unique specialty dishes
like Morgan Hill Retreat's *Diva Tomato Basil
Tart* or Jabberwock B&B's *Imperial Fiddle-
sticks*; or indulge in regional dishes like *Mon-
tana Potato Pie* from Bad Rock B&B, for a meal
not soon forgotten!

*All happiness
depends
on a leisurely
breakfast.*

JOHN GUNTHER

Eggs Benedict Caledonia

INGREDIENTS:

2 quality split English muffins

butter or spread

4 slices country ham (cooked)

4 eggs, poached

1 package hollandaise sauce mix

3 tbsp lemon juice, real or bottled

Caledonia Farm – 1812

47 Dearing Rd
Washington, VA 22627
800-BNB-1812
www.bnb1812.com

INSTRUCTIONS:

Toast or broil muffin halves and butter. Top with slices of ham. Warm at 160F in the oven. Poach eggs for 3 1/2 min in cups sprayed with vegetable oil. With whites set and yolks liquid, place inverted eggs upon muffins. Prepare hollandaise sauce, replacing 3 tbsp of water with lemon juice. Smother eggs with sauce. Decorate with fresh parsley, kiwi slice, strawberry half, or a favorite garnish of your choice. Practice this dish for confidence! The secret is flavorful ham and piquant hollandaise. Enjoy!

YIELD: *2 servings*
COOK TIME: *10 min*

Huevos Rancheros

INSTRUCTIONS:
Sauté green pepper, onion, mushrooms, tomato, and ham until tender, using olive oil or butter flavored vegetable oil. In the meantime, fold tortillas in half and spread 2 oz refried beans on each tortilla. Top with 2 oz cheese and place under broiler until cheese is melted and tortillas are slightly brown. Top with sautéed ingredients. Fry eggs over easy; place 2 eggs on top of each tortilla. Top with warm salsa, sour cream and 2 olives.

YIELD: *4 servings*
COOK TIME: *20 min*

INGREDIENTS:
1 green pepper, diced

1 small onion, diced

12 medium mushrooms, sliced

1 large ripe tomato, diced

8 oz lean ham, diced

4 8-inch tortillas

8 oz refried beans

8 oz shredded cheddar cheese

8 eggs

8 oz salsa (mild or medium)

4 oz sour cream

8 medium pitted black olives

Jackson Fork Inn, LLC
7345 East 900 S
Huntsville, UT 84317
801-745-0051
info@jacksonforkinn.com
www.jacksonforkinn.com

Oak Hill Eggs Benedict

Oak Hill on Love Lane

224 Love Ln
Waynesville, NC 28786
828-456-7037
oakhillonloveln@bell-south.net
www.oakhillonlovelane.com

INGREDIENTS:

HOLLANDAISE:

1 egg yolk

1 tbsp lemon juice

1/2 cup melted butter

Pinch salt and pepper

hot sauce (optional)

INSTRUCTIONS:

HOLLANDAISE

Combine egg yokes, lemon juice, salt and pepper in a blender, turn the blender on medium and drizzle the melted butter into the blender in a steady stream until the butter has emulsified into the eggs and is fully incorporated.

POTATO PANCAKES

Sauté onions in small amount of olive oil. In mixing bowl, lightly beat eggs. Add hash browns, matzo meal, sautéed onions, salt and pepper. Grease skillet with a combination of olive oil and butter. Deposit 1/4 cup batter into hot skillet and cook until golden brown. Do not disturb pancakes until they are ready to turn. Hold in a warm oven until ready to serve.

POACHED EGGS

Bring approximately 5 cups of water to a light boil and add vinegar and a pinch of salt. Break each egg into a small cup or bowl and gently slide into the water. Add each additional egg, making sure not to crowd the pan. Cook to desired doneness, approximately 3 min for soft yolks. Remove with slotted spoon.

ASSEMBLY

Place 2 potato pancakes on plate. Top each with slice of smoked salmon, then a poached egg. Add hollandaise sauce and sprinkle with smoked paprika. Garnish plate with sliced tomato and capers.

YIELD: *4 servings*

POTATO PANCAKES:

1/2 cup onion, chopped

4 cups hash browns

1/2 cup matzo meal

2 large eggs

Pinch salt and pepper

POACHED EGGS:

8 large eggs

1 tbsp vinegar

PRESENTATION:

8 oz smoked salmon, sliced

1 large tomato, sliced

capers

smoked paprika

Maple Baked Eggs

INGREDIENTS:

1 tbsp butter

1 tbsp maple syrup

2 slices white bread

2 medium eggs

INSTRUCTIONS:

Melt butter, add maple syrup, and stir. Trim crusts from bread. Slather butter/maple syrup mixture on one side of each slice of bread. Place each slice in a well-greased muffin tin, folding as necessary. Break an egg into each. Bake at 425F for about 10 min, until just firm.

YIELD: *2 servings*
COOK TIME: *10 min*

The Governor's House in Hyde Park

100 Main St
Hyde Park, VT 05655
866-800-6888
info@OneHundredMain.com
www.OneHundredMain.com

Sourdough Eggs

INSTRUCTIONS:

Cut bread into small cubes. Place 1/2 of bread cubes into large coated baking dish. Sprinkle with 2 cups cheese, onion, and mushrooms. Add second layer of bread and top with remaining cheese. Beat eggs, milk, mustard, salt and pepper together. Pour this mixture evenly over the casserole. Cover with foil and refrigerate overnight. Bake at 325F for approximately 50 min until top is golden and lightly crusted.

YIELD: *6 servings*
COOK TIME: *50 min*

INGREDIENTS:

12 slices of lightly buttered extra-sour sourdough bread

4 cups grated cheddar cheese

1/2 medium onion, diced

1 cup thinly sliced mushrooms

10 eggs

4 cups milk

3 heaping tbsp of spicy mustard

1 tsp salt

1/4 tsp pepper

The Wine Country Inn & Gardens

1152 Lodi Ln
St. Helena, CA 94574
888-465-4608
jim@winecountryinn.com
www.winecountryinn.com

Crème Caramel Over-Night French Toast

INGREDIENTS:

1/4 cup butter

1/2 cup light corn syrup

1 cup brown sugar

1 loaf French bread, cut into 9 pieces

1 1/2 cups eggs, beaten

2 1/2 cups nonfat milk

1/3 cup sugar

1 tbsp cinnamon

1 1/2 tsp ground allspice

1 tbsp vanilla extract

INSTRUCTIONS:

Before preparing mixture, melt butter and corn syrup together in a small saucepan. Then stir in brown sugar and bring to a rolling boil. Let boil for 1 to 2 min. Pour the hot caramel into a buttered 9 1/2x13-inch baking pan and chill in refrigerator for 10 to 20 min or until set. Next, slice French bread and arrange gently on top of caramel. Mix all remaining ingredients and pour carefully over bread. Cover and refrigerate overnight. The next day, preheat oven to 350F. Bake until set, approximately 1 hr. When serving, flip pieces over onto the plate so the melted caramel sauce drips down all over the French toast. Top with fresh fruit and a dollop of low fat yogurt.

YIELD: *9 servings*
COOK TIME: *1 hr*

Beazley House
1910 1st Street
Napa, CA 94559
800-559-1649
innkeeper@beazleyhouse.com
www.beazleyhouse.com

Upside-Down Apple French Toast

INSTRUCTIONS:

Combine butter, brown sugar and water in a saucepan. Heat on medium until bubbling, stirring frequently. Place in a 9x13-inch pan and allow to cool for 20–30 min. Peel, core and slice the apples. Place the slices in rows, close together (overlapping), on top of the sauce in the pan. Sprinkle with cinnamon. Place the slices of bread on top of the apples. Mix together the milk, eggs and vanilla. Pour over the bread. Sprinkle with a little nutmeg. Cover and refrigerate. Bake at 350F for approximately 60 min, or until golden brown and crispy on top. Serve upside-down. Spoon the sauce in the pan over the French toast. Garnish with almonds.

YIELD: *8 servings*
COOK TIME: *60 min*

INGREDIENTS:

1/2 cup (1 stick) butter

1¼ cup packed brown sugar

1 tsp water

3 Granny Smith apples

cinnamon, to taste

1 loaf French bread, sliced 1½ inches thick

1½ cup milk

6 large eggs

1 tsp vanilla

nutmeg, to taste

sliced almonds, for garnish

Captain Wohlt Inn
123 E 3rd St
Hermann, MO 65041
573-486-3357
captainwohltinn@gmail.com
www.captainwohltbandb.com

Macadamia-Banana French Toast

INGREDIENTS:

1 banana, sliced

1 cup milk

4 eggs

3½ oz macadamia nuts, chopped well

1 tsp vanilla extract

dash cinnamon or allspice

8–10 slices whole wheat bread

powdered sugar for dusting

1 banana, sliced for garnish

INSTRUCTIONS:
Preheat oven to 475F.

Blend together, in blender or food processor, one banana, milk, eggs, half the chopped nuts, vanilla and cinnamon, until well mixed. Pour into large, shallow dish. Dip bread slices into mixture until well absorbed on both sides. Arrange on 2 large, well-buttered baking sheets. Bake until golden, flipping over half way through, about 5 min on each side.

Remove from baking sheets. Slice diagonally and dust with powdered sugar. Top with remaining banana and chopped nuts.

YIELD: *4 servings*
COOK TIME: *10 min*

Howard Creek Ranch
40501 N Hwy 1
Westport, CA 95488
707-964-6725
howardcreekranch@mcn.org
www.howardcreekranch.com

Pecan and Wild Maine Blueberry French Toast

INSTRUCTIONS:
Preheat oven to 325F.

Spread the bread cubes in a baking pan (ungreased) and bake for 15 min until golden and slightly toasted. Pull out of oven to cool.

Butter a 13x9-inch baking dish with the single tbsp of butter, and pack the dried bread cubes into it. Whisk the eggs in a large bowl until combined. Then whisk in the milk, cream, granulated sugar, vanilla, cinnamon, and nutmeg. Pour the egg mixture over the bread cubes. Cover the entire mixture with plastic wrap and press the bread down into the egg mixture so it is soft and well coated. Refrigerate overnight.

To make the topping, stir the 4 tbsp butter, brown sugar, and corn syrup together until smooth and then stir in the pecans. Wrap in plastic wrap and also refrigerate overnight. The next day, preheat the oven to 350F. Unwrap the casserole and bake for 45 min. Remove and sprinkle the blueberries on top, then add the pecan topping mixture and bake for another 15 min until golden brown and bubbling. Serve immediately with warmed maple syrup.

YIELD: *12 servings*
COOK TIME: *1 hr*

The Buttonwood Inn
64 Mount Surprise Rd
North Conway, NH 03860
800-258-2625
innkeeper@buttonwoodinn.com
www.buttonwoodinn.com

INGREDIENTS:

1 16-oz loaf French or Italian bread, cut into 1" cubes

1 tbsp unsalted butter, soft

8 large eggs

2½ cups whole milk

1½ cups heavy cream

1 tbsp granulated sugar

2 tsp vanilla extract

1/2 tsp ground cinnamon

1/2 tsp ground nutmeg

4 tbsp unsalted butter, soft

3/4 cup packed light brown sugar

1½ tbsp light corn syrup

1 cup pecans, coarse chopped

1 cup wild Maine or regular blueberries

Banana French Toast *with Raspberry Coulis*

INGREDIENTS:

FILLING:

4 oz cream cheese

2 ripe bananas

1 tbsp powdered sugar

8 slices thick Texas toast

EGG DIP:

4 eggs

1 cup half & half

1/4 cup sugar

1 tbsp banana extract or liquor

chocolate sauce

raspberry coulis

The Kingsleigh Inn
373 Main St
Southwest Harbor, ME 04679
207-244-5302
relax@kingsleighinn.com
www.kingsleighinn.com

INSTRUCTIONS:

Mash the filling ingredients and spread on 4 bread slices. Place 2nd piece of bread on top.

Beat eggs, half & half, sugar and extract in bowl. Dip "sandwiches" into mixture, and flip to ensure even soaking. Fry both sides on medium hot griddle until nicely browned. Place on baking sheet and cover and bake at 325F for 20 min.

To serve, cut in half and dust with powdered sugar. Here at the inn we serve the French toast on a Raspberry Coulis (which is puréed and strained raspberries, lemon juice and powdered sugar) with a dark chocolate drizzle (which unfortunately is a secret recipe!) BUT, there are numerous sauces available at markets and gourmet purveyors. It's basically a melted chocolate with cream recipe.

YIELD: *4 servings*
COOK TIME: *20 min*

Caramel Pecan French Toast

INGREDIENTS:

- 3/4 cup butter
- 1½ cups packed brown sugar
- 1/3 cup light corn syrup
- 3/4 cup chopped pecans
- 12 thick slices French or Challah bread
- 2½ cups whole milk
- 4 eggs, beaten
- 1 tbsp vanilla extract
- 1/4 tsp salt
- 1½ tsp cinnamon
- 3 tbsp granulated sugar
- 1/4 cup butter, melted

INSTRUCTIONS:

Combine butter, brown sugar and corn syrup in medium saucepan. Cook over medium heat, stirring constantly until bubbly, 5 min. Pour syrup evenly into greased 9x13-inch baking dish. Sprinkle with pecans. Arrange bread over pecans. Combine milk, eggs, vanilla, and salt. Stir well and pour over bread. Cover and chill at least 8 hrs.

Remove from refrigerator and sprinkle with mixture of cinnamon and sugar. Drizzle with melted butter. Bake uncovered at 350F for 45–50 min or until golden and bubbly.

YIELD: *10 servings*
COOK TIME: *45–50 min*

The Red Rocker Inn

136 N Dougherty St
Black Mountain, NC 28711
888-669-5991
info@redrockerinn.com
www.redrockerinn.com

Banana's Foster French Toast

INGREDIENTS:

1½–2 loaves
French Bread

16 oz cream
cheese (softened)

2–4 ripe bananas

1/4 cup dark rum

2½ cup whipping
cream or heavy
cream, split

10 large eggs,
beaten

1 tsp vanilla

1/4 tsp nutmeg

1 cup pecan pieces
(chopped)

cinnamon

brown sugar

powdered sugar,
for garnish

CARAMEL SYRUP:

1 stick butter

1¾ cup light
brown sugar

pinch of salt

1 cup heavy cream

INSTRUCTIONS:

Spray 2 9x13-inch baking dishes. Slice bread half inch thick. Layer bottom of each dish with French bread (tightly). Fill in empty spaces with cut sections of bread.

BANANA FILLING:

Purée cream cheese in food processor, add bananas and rum, purée again. Add 1½ cups whipping cream while blending. Split the filling over the 2 pans of bread.

EGG MIXTURE:

Beat eggs, 1 cup whipping cream, vanilla, and nutmeg. Place another layer of bread; then pour egg mixture over second layer of bread. Sprinkle with pecans pieces, cinnamon and brown sugar. Refrigerate overnight. Bake at 350F for 25–35 min or until set and brown.

Top with sliced bananas, caramel syrup, and dust with powdered sugar.

CARAMEL SYRUP

Combine all ingredients in sauce pan and bring to rolling boil; stirring constantly for about 1½ to 2 min until thickened.

YIELD: *18 servings*
COOK TIME: *25–35 min*

**Two Meeting Street
Inn B&B**

2 Meeting St, Charleston, SC 29401
888-723-7322
innkeeper2meetst@bellsouth.net
www.twomeetingstreet.com

Maple Baked Pancake

INSTRUCTIONS:
Preheat oven to 350F.

Brown enough link sausages to cover bottom of 9-inch pan, then drain fat well.

Arrange cooked sausage in bottom of pan. Mix sufficient pancake mix according to package directions and pour over sausages to no more than about 1/3 of the depth of the selected pan (it will rise). Bake for 45 min (cooking time may vary with oven).

Test with toothpick to make sure it is almost cooked—toothpick should come out dry. Poke holes in raised pancake. Drizzle caramel sauce over pancakes, if desired. Sprinkle pecan pieces on top, if desired. Put pan back in oven to warm sauce Slice into 3x3-inch squares to serve. Serve with maple syrup and butter.

YIELD: *9 servings*
COOK TIME: *45 min*

INGREDIENTS:

brown-n-serve sausage (pork or turkey; suggest pre-cooked and maple flavored)

pancake mix (regular or buttermilk)

pecan pieces, optional

caramel sauce

Inn at Aberdeen, Ltd.
1758 Clifty Creek Ct
Valparaiso, IN 46385
866-761-3753
inn@innataberdeen.com
www.innataberdeen.com

Baked Pear Pancakes

INGREDIENTS:

6 eggs

1 cup whole milk

1 cup flour

4 tbsp melted butter

1/2 tsp almond extract

2 tsp lemon zest

3 large pears (1/2 per dish), preferably Bosc pears

2 tbsp powdered sugar

3 tbsp lemon juice

Old Monterey Inn
500 Martin St
Monterey, CA 93940
800-350-2344
omi@oldmontereyinn.com
www.oldmontereyinn.com

NOTE: *These pancakes can be made without layering the fruit before baking. The sides of the casserole will force the edges of the batter up. The pancakes will stay formed and can be filled with any seasonal fruit.*

INSTRUCTIONS:

In a blender or bowl, mix eggs and milk. Stir in flour. While stirring, add melted butter. Add the extract and zest. (Mixture may be made the evening before and refrigerated. Let it come to room temperature before using.) Preheat oven to 425F. Peel and core the pears. Halve the pears and slice. Mix the sugar and lemon juice in a bowl. Toss the sliced pears in the juice mixture. Layer one half pear (5 or 6 slices) into each of 6 individual gratin dishes, or one large casserole dish, greased. Pour 1/2 cup of the batter over the pears. Bake 20 min. When baked, sprinkle with powdered sugar; decorate with fresh berries or seasonal fruit. Pass additional fresh fruit and syrup if desired.

YIELD: *6 servings*
COOK TIME: *20 min*

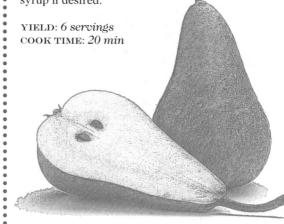

Orange Pancakes

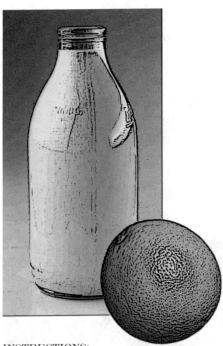

INGREDIENTS:

BATTER:

2 cups "JIFFY" Baking Mix

1 egg

1 cup milk

1/2 cup orange juice

1 tbsp orange rind

SAUCE:

1/4 cup butter

1/3 cup orange juice

1/4 cup sugar

1/2 tsp vanilla

1 tsp orange rind

INSTRUCTIONS:

Mix all batter ingredients in large bowl. Ladle mix onto large pan or skillet by the scoopful. Allow pancakes to bubble, then flip.

Combine ingredients for sauce in small pan and cook on medium heat until sauce simmers. Serve pancakes with sauce on top or on the side, with a garnish of orange rinds.

YIELD: *4–6 servings*

Banana Pancakes with *Toffee Nut Sauce*

INGREDIENTS:

2 cups all-purpose baking mix

1/2 cup milk

1/2 cup plain yogurt

2 eggs

2 ripe bananas, sliced 1/4" thick

SAUCE:

1/2 cup *each* unsalted butter, packed brown sugar, and light corn syrup

1/4 cup heavy cream

1/2 cup walnuts, chopped

INSTRUCTIONS:

Stir milk, yogurt, and eggs together with baking mix until blended. Pour 1/4 cup batter onto a hot griddle. Press banana slices into each pancake. Cook until edges are dry, flip and cook until golden.

To make sauce, put all 5 ingredients into a saucepan and heat gently, stirring constantly until sugar has dissolved. Boil for 3 min and serve immediately, pouring the sauce over the pancakes. The sauce will solidify when cool.

YIELD: *1 dozen*

Addison On Amelia

614 Ash St
Amelia Island, FL 32034
800-943-1604
info@AddisonOnAmelia.com
www.AddisonOnAmelia.com

Apple Oat Cakes

INGREDIENTS:

2 cups rolled oats

1 cup flour

2 tbsp sugar

1 tsp baking powder

1 tsp baking soda

1 minced apple

1 tbsp cinnamon

1/2 tsp ginger

1/2 tsp nutmeg

2 cups buttermilk

2 eggs

INSTRUCTIONS:
Mix all ingredients and pour by 1/4 cupfuls onto hot griddle or on baking sheet to bake in oven for 10 min.

Makes approximately 24 oat cakes. May be stored in refrigerator and heated in oven or toaster.

YIELD: *2 dozen*
COOK TIME: *10 min*

Asa Ransom House
10529 Main St, Rt 5
Clarence, NY 14031
800-841-2340
innfo@asaransom.com
www.asaransom.com

Apple German Pancake

INGREDIENTS:

1/2 cup butter
(1 stick)

3 apples peeled
and thinly sliced

1 tbsp sugar

BATTER:

1 cup "JIFFY"
Baking Mix

1/4 tsp cinnamon

1/2 cup sugar

6 eggs

1 cup milk

1 tsp vanilla

INSTRUCTIONS:

Place butter in 9x13-inch dish and put in oven
while it is preheating to 400F.

Add 1 tbsp of sugar to apples and place in dish.
Stir apples to coat in butter. Cook for 10 min.

While apples are cooking, mix all dry batter ingredients. Add the liquid batter ingredients and
blend on medium speed for 4 min.

Pour batter onto cooked apples. Cook for 20
min.

Sprinkle with powdered cinnamon-sugar.

YIELD: *8–10 servings*
COOK TIME: *30 min*

Gingerbread Pancakes

INGREDIENTS:

- 2 1/2 cups all-purpose flour
- 5 tsp baking powder
- 1 1/2 tsp salt
- 1 tsp baking soda
- 1 tsp cinnamon
- 1/2 tsp ginger
- 1/4 cup molasses
- 2 cups milk
- 2 eggs, lightly beaten
- 6 tbsp butter, melted
- 1 cup raisins

INSTRUCTIONS:

Sift together flour, baking powder, salt, soda and spices. In separate bowl, combine molasses and milk and add eggs, blending to stiffen. Stir in melted butter. Add molasses mixture to dry ingredients. Stir only until moistened. Mix in raisins. Cook on a hot griddle, using 1/4 cup batter for each pancake.

YIELD: *2 dozen*

Hersey House & Bungalow
451 N Main St
Ashland, OR 97520
888-343-7739
innkeeper@herseyhouse.com
www.herseyhouse.com

Carrot Cake Pancakes

INGREDIENTS:

2½ cups all-purpose flour

4 tbsp finely chopped pecans

4 tsp baking powder

2 tsp ground cinnamon

1/2 tsp salt

1/2 tsp ground ginger

dash nutmeg

2 eggs, lightly beaten

2/3 cup packed brown or granulated sugar

2¼ cups milk

2 cups *each* finely grated carrots and golden raisins

8 oz soft cream cheese

1/2 cup powdered sugar

1/3 cup milk

1 tsp vanilla

dash ground cinnamon

INSTRUCTIONS:

In a bowl, combine flour, pecans, baking powder, cinnamon, salt, ginger, and nutmeg. In a separate bowl, combine eggs, sugar, milk, carrots, and raisins; mix well. Stir carrot mixture into dry ingredients until moistened.

Pour batter by 1/4 cupful onto a greased hot griddle. When bubbles form on the top of pancakes; flip and continue to cook until golden brown. For topping, blend cream cheese, powdered sugar, milk and vanilla until smooth. Sprinkle with cinnamon, and serve with pancakes.

YIELD: *6 servings*

The Barn Inn
6838 CR 203
Millersburg, OH 44654
877-674-7600
reservations@thebarninn.com
www.thebarninn.com

Lemon-Cornmeal Blueberry Pancakes

INGREDIENTS:

- 3 cups flour
- 4 1/2 cups cornmeal
- 6 tbsp sugar
- 6 tsp baking powder
- 1 1/2 tsp baking soda
- 1 1/2 tsp salt
- 3 large eggs
- 6 cups buttermilk
- 9 tbsp unsalted butter, melted and cooled slightly
- 6 tsp lemon zest
- 3 cups blueberries

Captain Jefferds Inn
5 Pearl St
Kennebunkport, ME 04046
800-839-6844
captjeff@captainjef-
ferdsinn.com
www.captainjefferdsinn.com

INSTRUCTIONS:

Mix together flour, cornmeal, sugar, baking powder, baking soda, and salt. In a separate bowl, whisk eggs, milk, melted butter, and lemon zest. Combine dry and liquid ingredients. Do not over mix, a few lumps should remain.

Fold blueberries gently into mixture or sprinkle 1 tbsp blueberries over each pancake. Cook pancakes to golden brown.

YIELD: *18 servings*

Blue Corn Waffles

Hacienda Nicholas B&B

320 E Marcy St
Santa Fe, NM 87501
888-284-3170
info@haciendanicholas.com
www.haciendanicholas.com

INGREDIENTS:

1 cup whole wheat flour

1½ cups blue corn-meal

2½ tbsp white sugar

2 tbsp baking powder

3/4 tsp baking soda

1¾ cups nonfat buttermilk

4 egg whites

INSTRUCTIONS:

Preheat a waffle iron and coat with cooking spray. In a medium bowl, stir together the whole wheat flour, cornmeal, sugar, baking powder and baking soda. Make a well in the center, and stir in the buttermilk just until smooth. In a separate bowl, whip egg whites with an electric mixer until thick enough to hold a soft peak. Carefully fold the egg whites into the batter.

Spoon batter onto the hot waffle iron in an amount appropriate for your iron. Close and cook until the iron stops steaming, and the waffles are golden brown.

YIELD: *8 large waffles*

Apple Cranberry Baked Oatmeal

INGREDIENTS:

2/3 cup
vegetable oil

1 cup brown sugar

2 eggs

2 tsp baking
powder

1 tsp salt

3 cups raw oats

1 cup milk

2 cups apples,
diced

1 cup dried
cranberries

INSTRUCTIONS:
Preheat oven to 350F.

Mix oil, sugar, eggs, baking powder and salt together until smooth. Stir in oatmeal and milk.
Mix until combined. Spray a 9x13-inch pan and
layer in apples and cranberries. Pour oatmeal
mixture over fruit.

Bake for 30 min or until top is golden brown.

YIELD: *9 servings*
COOK TIME: *30 min*

St. Francis Inn
279 St George St
St. Augustine, FL 32084
800-824-6062
info@stfrancisinn.com
www.stfrancisinn.com

DREAMCATCHER
Hot Oats Brulée

INGREDIENTS:

1/2 cup Irish Steel cut oats

1/2 cup Quaker-type slow cooking oats

small handful of sliced almonds

small handful of raisins

1 cup milk

1 cup water

dash of salt

INSTRUCTIONS:

Mix oats, almonds and raisins. Heat up the milk and water with salt. Once very warm, add the mixture and stir regularly so it does not stick to the bottom of the pan.

Put cooked oats into a small ramekin. Sprinkle 1 spoonful of raw sugar on top. Use a torch and brulee the raw sugar. Put a dollop of sour cream and top it off with a raspberry or strawberry.

YIELD: *6 servings*
COOK TIME: *20 min*

Dream-catcher

416 La Lomita Rd
Taos, NM 87571
888-758-0613
dream@taosnm.com
www.dreambb.com

Apple Cinnamon Oatmeal Casserole

INSTRUCTIONS:
Preheat oven to 350F.

Grease medium casserole dish. Combine milk, brown sugar, butter and salt in a saucepan over medium heat. Bring to simmer, cook until butter is melted. Remove from heat. Put oats in casserole. Stir in milk mixture, cinnamon, nutmeg, apple, nuts, raisins, and cranberries. Bake for 20–30 min. Serve with milk or cream.

YIELD: *4 servings*
COOK TIME: *20–30 min*

INGREDIENTS:

2 cups milk

1/4 cup packed brown sugar

2 tbsp butter

1/2 tsp salt

1 cup old fashioned oats

2 tsp cinnamon

1 tsp nutmeg

2 finely chopped apples, skins on or peeled

1/2 cup sliced almonds

1/2 cup raisins, golden preferred

1/2 cup sweetened, dried cranberries

Australian Walkabout Inn
837 Village Rd
Lancaster, PA 17602
888-WALK-ABT
stay@walkaboutinn.com
www.walkaboutinn.com

Tootie's Granola

INGREDIENTS:

2 cups oatmeal

1 cup wheat germ, optional

1 cup coconut

1 cup sunflower seeds, raw and unsalted)

1/2 cup sesame seeds

1 tbsp vanilla

1/2 cup vegetable oil

2/3 cup honey

1/2 cup water

1 cup nuts (pecans, almonds, walnuts, etc., or a mix)

NOTE: *If, after baking, the granola looks done, it is probably too done. Normally the first time one makes it, it is baked too long, and is dry rather than moist. It's still good, but is even better moist.*

INSTRUCTIONS:
Preheat oven to 350F. Mix all dry ingredients well. Combine warm water, oil, honey, and vanilla. Pour over dry ingredients and stir. Bake for 40 min, stirring every 10 min to prevent over-browning on top. For a moist granola (like ours) bake in a deep dish pan, with granola about 2 inches thick. Store in a tightly sealed container.

YIELD: *16 servings*
COOK TIME: *40 min*

A Teton Tree House
6175 Heck of a Hill Rd, Jackson, WY 83014
307-733-3233
atetontreehouse@aol.com
www.atetontreehouse-jacksonhole.com

Breakfast Enchiladas

INSTRUCTIONS:

Grease a 9x13-inch baking dish. In a skillet over medium-high heat, cook the sausage, onion and carrot, crumbling the meat while cooking, until cooked; cool completely.

Place about 1/3 cup of the cooked sausage mixture down the center of each tortilla, and sprinkle each with 2 tbsp cheese. Roll up each tortilla and place seam-side down into the casserole dish. In a bowl, whisk the eggs with flour, half and half, cayenne and black pepper. Pour over the top of the tortillas. Sprinkle about 1 1/2 cups of shredded cheese on top. Cover with foil and refrigerate for 1 hour or overnight.

The next day, preheat oven to 350F. Remove from the refrigerator 45 min before baking. With foil cover still in place, bake for 35 min, then uncover and continue to bake for another 15 min. Let stand 15 min before serving. Garnish.

YIELD: *10 servings*
COOK TIME: *50 min*

INGREDIENTS:

1 lb turkey sausage

1 onion, finely chopped

1 carrot, finely chopped

10 8-inch flour tortillas

1¼ cups grated cheddar cheese

6 large eggs or 1½ cups egg whites

1 tbsp flour

2 cups half and half

1 pinch cayenne or white pepper

1 tsp fresh ground black pepper (or to taste)

sour cream and salsa for garnish

Night Swan Intracoastal B&B

512 S Riverside Dr
New Smyrna Beach, FL 32168
800-465-4261
info@NightSwan.com
www.NightSwan.com

Country-Style Turkey Sausage Patties

INGREDIENTS:

1 slightly beaten egg white

1/4 cup finely chopped onion

1/2 cup finely chopped apple

3 tbsp quick-cooking oats

2 tbsp fresh parsley

1/2 tsp salt

1/2 tsp ground sage

1/4 tsp ground nutmeg

1/4 tsp pepper

1/8 tsp ground red pepper

8 oz lean ground turkey breast

INSTRUCTIONS:

Combine egg white, onion, apples, oats, parsley, salt, sage, nutmeg, pepper and red pepper in a medium bowl. Add turkey and mix well. Shape mixture into eight 2-inch diameter patties.

Coat skillet with non-stick spray and place over medium heat. Cook patties 10–12 min or until meat is no longer pink and juices run clear, turning once. Drain off fat.

YIELD: *6 servings*
COOK TIME: *10–12 min*

Gansevoort House Inn

42 W Gansevoort St
Little Falls, NY 13365
315-823-3969
info@gansevoorthouse.com
www.gansevoorthouse.com

Power-Pack Breakfast Casserole

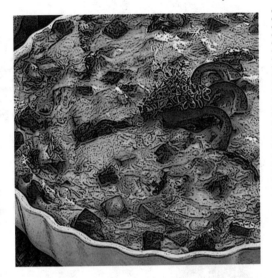

INGREDIENTS:

4 eggs

1 cup "JIFFY" Baking Mix

1/2 cup milk

1 cup of cottage cheese

1 cup grated cheese (cheddar, jack or Swiss)

1/4 finely diced onion

1 cup cubed ham

2 cups frozen hash browns

pepper

INSTRUCTIONS:
Beat eggs, baking mix and milk on medium speed for 2 min.

Add the remaining ingredients and stir well. Pour into 8x8-inch prepared dish.

Cook for 45–50 min at 350F.

YIELD: *6 servings*
COOK TIME: *45–50 min*

THE MAPLE LEAF INN
Breakfast Pizza

The Maple Leaf Inn

5890 Vermont Rt 12

Barnard, VT 05031

800-516-2753

innkeeper@mapleleafinn.com

www.mapleleafinn.com

NOTE: *The dough can be made in advance. Once it has risen, it can be frozen and then thawed in the refrigerator and brought to room temperature over several hours. It needs to be warm and pliable to form the pizzas.*

INSTRUCTIONS:

To make the crust, put the flour, salt, and yeast in a food processor fitted with the dough blade and pulse several times to mix. With the processor running, add the tablespoon of oil through the feeding chute. Then add the water in a stream until a soft ball forms—you will typically not use the entire cup. Stop the processor and move the dough to a floured surface. Knead a couple of times and then form into a ball. Put the

dough in a small oiled bowl and cover tightly with plastic wrap and put in a warm place to rise for 1½ to 2 hrs—until doubled.

About an hour before baking the pizzas, pre-heat the oven with a pizza stone to 480F. When the rising is done, take the dough from the bowl and place it on a lightly floured surface. Cut into 4 equal portions and form them into tight individual balls. Put a little olive oil on each and lightly cover with plastic wrap. Let them rest for about 10 min.

When ready to form the pizzas, take each ball and gently pull it into a small round crust. Then, place on parchment paper. Dimple the crust with your finger tips and using the heel of your hand, push the crust into a larger circle with the outer edge a bit higher than the middle—each crust will be approximately 6 inches in diameter.

Brush a little olive oil on each crust and sprinkle the diced ham on each, leaving an empty spot in the middle of the crust. Place three tomato slices on top of the ham. Then sprinkle the cheese on top of the ham and tomatoes. All these ingredients should form a dam to hold the egg in place. Place the parchment with the pizzas on the preheated stone and slide a raw egg into the middle of each pizza. Bake for about 8–10 min – until the egg whites are set and the crust turns a golden brown. Remove from the oven, and slide onto a plate and serve while hot.

YIELD: *4 pizzas*
COOK TIME: *8–10 min*

INGREDIENTS:

2 cups unbleached bread flour

1 tsp salt

1 tsp fast-rising (bread machine) yeast

1 tbsp olive oil, plus extra for the oiling the bowl

1 cup warm water (not hot)

1 cup diced ham

12 thin slices tomato

3/4 cup grated Parmesan cheese

4 large eggs, broken into individual bowls (yokes intact)

The Pond's Mexicali Frittata

INGREDIENTS:

2 lbs ground sausage

12 large eggs

1/3 cup heavy cream

salt and pepper to taste

1 medium onion, diced

1 tbsp butter

5–6 pieces wheat bread

12 oz Mexican blend shredded cheese

7 oz can diced green chili

1/8 cup chopped cilantro

1/2 cup medium salsa

INSTRUCTIONS:

Remove sausage from casing and brown sausage in skillet. Set aside sausage, draining rendered fat. In separate bowl, beat eggs, cream, salt and pepper until well mixed. Sauté onion in butter until soft.

Line bottom of 9x13-inch baking pan with wheat bread, spread sausage evenly over bread and sprinkle with 1/3 of the cheese. Combine onion, green chilies and spread evenly over casserole. Spread 1/3 of remaining cheese over casserole. Pour egg mixture evenly over casserole. Top with all but 2 tbsp of remaining cheese. Cover with aluminum foil and store in refrigerator overnight.

Bake at 350F for 45–55 min until all liquid has been absorbed and top is slightly hard to the touch. Sprinkle with remaining cheese and let set for 10 min. Slice and garnish with cilantro stalk and salsa. Serve warm. Goes great with toast and fresh tomatoes or fruit!

YIELD: *10 servings*
COOK TIME: *45–55 min*

Pearson's Pond
Luxury Inn
and Adventure Spa
4541 Sawa Circle
Juneau, AK 99801
888-658-6328
pearsonspond@gci.net
www.pearsonspond.com

Salsa Soufflé

INGREDIENTS:

1 tbsp salsa

1/4 cup cheese, grated

cooked bacon (optional)

chives (optional)

1 egg

1/3 cup milk

INSTRUCTIONS:

Preheat oven to 350F. Coat a 3½-inch ramekin with oil. Place 1 tbsp salsa in ramekin to cover bottom of dish. Top with grated cheese. Add cooked bacon or chives, if desired. (Dish should be about 3/4 full now.) Beat egg together with milk. Pour into ramekin. Bake 1 hr. Take out of oven and serve immediately.

YIELD: *1 serving*
COOK TIME: *1 hr*

Fensalden Inn
33810 Navarro Ridge Rd
Albion, CA 95410
800-959-3850
inn@fensalden.com
www.fensalden.com

Imperial Fiddlesticks

INGREDIENTS:

15 eggs

2 lbs cottage cheese (approx. 4½ cups)

2½ tbsp baking powder

2¼ cups flour

2½ cups milk

salt to taste

1 lb *each* pepper jack, mozzarella, and cheddar cheeses (approx. 4 cups each, grated)

1/2 lb cream cheese (approx 8 oz)

1 bunch cilantro

1 tomato

1 avocado

frozen corn

1 jalapeño (no seeds)

1/4 red onion

1 mango

salt and pepper to taste

Above: Breakfast at the Jabberwock B&B. Photo by Innlight Marketing.

INSTRUCTIONS:
Preheat oven to 350F. To make soufflé, mix eggs, cottage cheese, baking powder, flour, milk and salt. Add cheeses and mix well. Spray ramekins with non-stick spray and pour in mixture. Bake for approximately 1 hr.

To make salsa, chop all fruits and vegetables (except corn). Mix all ingredients well. Serve on top of the soufflé.

YIELD: *15 servings*
COOK TIME: *1 hr*

Jabberwock B&B
598 Laine St, Monterey, CA 93940
888-428-7253
innkeeper@jabberwockinn.com
www.jabberwockinn.com

Hash Brown Quiche

INSTRUCTIONS:

Preheat oven to 450F. If using frozen hash brown potatoes, thaw, then press the drained hash browns between paper towels to dry them as best as possible. In a 9-inch pie plate, toss the hash browns with the melted butter. Press them into the bottom and up the sides to form a crust. Bake for 20–25 min until golden brown and starting to crisp. Lower the oven temperature to 350F.

Meanwhile, in a large mixing bowl, combine the remaining ingredients, except for the spinach. When the hash brown crust is ready, layer spinach leaves in the bottom. Pour the egg mixture over it and return the plate to the oven. Bake at 350F for 30 min or until the quiche is light and golden brown and the top has puffed.

Let rest for 5 min before serving.

YIELD: 6 *servings*
COOK TIME: 50–55 *min*

INGREDIENTS:

3 cups shredded potatoes, uncooked

4 tbsp butter, melted

3 large eggs, beaten

1 cup half and half

1/2 cup green onions

1 cup sharp cheddar, shredded

1/4 cup red bell pepper, chopped

spinach leaves

Red Bud Manor
7 Kings Hwy
Eureka Springs, AR 72632
479-253-9649
redbudmanor@cox-internet.com
www.redbudmanorinn.com

Greek Vegetarian Quiche

INGREDIENTS:

1 unbaked 9" pie crust

8 oz frozen chopped spinach

1 tsp butter

1 tsp olive oil

3 tbsp minced white onion

1 clove minced garlic or dash of garlic powder

1 1/2 cup grated light flavored cheese like mozzarella

1/4 cup crumbled feta cheese (or more if desired)

1 1/2 cup heavy cream, half and half, or combination of the two

4 large eggs, beaten

1/8 tsp fresh grated nutmeg

1/4 tsp salt

1/8 tsp fresh ground pepper

INSTRUCTIONS:

Shape pie crust in a deep quiche dish or pie pan. Defrost frozen spinach and squeeze as dry as possible.

Preheat oven to 400F. Melt butter and oil in small skillet. Sauté onion and garlic over med heat until onion is translucent. Add spinach and sauté for 2 more min. Let cool slightly—about 10 min.

Sprinkle about 1/2 cup mozzarella over crust. Spread spinach/onion over cheese. Crumble feta over onion and sprinkle remaining mozzarella.

Beat cream, eggs, nutmeg, salt and pepper together with whisk. Pour over pie crust slowly so all liquid is absorbed. Grate a bit of nutmeg over the top for added color.

Bake for 35–40 min until quiche is puffy and golden and center does not seem liquid when moved. Allow to cool at least 10–15 min before cutting.

YIELD: *6–8 portions depending on hunger factor!*
COOK TIME: *35–40 min*

Carlisle House B&B

148 S Hanover St
Carlisle, PA 17013
717-249-0350
stay@thecarlislehouse.com
www.thecarlislehouse.com

Isaiah's Incredible Quiche

Isaiah Clark House

1187 Main St
Brewster, MA 02631
800-822-4001
stay@isaiahclark.com
www.isaiahclark.com

INGREDIENTS:

9" pie crust
(homemade or
readymade)

3½ cups of
shredded Monterey
Jack cheese

1¾ cups of
shredded Cheddar
cheese

handful of fresh
basil, parsley, or
other fresh herbs

4 eggs

1 cup of half and
half (or 1/2 cup
each of milk and
half and half)

dash nutmeg,
or to taste

pinch of salt and
pepper

INSTRUCTIONS:

Preheat oven to 375F.

Prepare and roll piecrust. Arrange in 9-inch pie
pan, roll excess up to edge, and flute. Mix
cheeses together by tossing lightly until the mix
is even. Put the cheeses and herbs into the raw
pie shell and spread so the shell is full to just
below the fluted edge. Beat eggs, half and half,
nutmeg, and salt and pepper. Pour egg mixture
into crust until the cheese is just covered. (Do
not overfill or the quiche will overflow when
cooking.) If there is not enough liquid, add
more half and half until the desired fullness is
achieved.

Bake for 1 hr or until a toothpick comes out
dry. Allow 5 min before cutting and serving.

YIELD: *6 servings*
COOK TIME: *1 hr*

Three-Cheese Quiche

INSTRUCTIONS:
Preheat oven to 350F.

In a large bowl, combine the eggs, egg yolks, whipping cream, half and half, mozzarella cheese, 1/2 cup cheddar cheese, Swiss cheese, tomatoes, seasoning blend and basil; pour into a greased quiche pan (or a 9-inch deep dish pie plate). Sprinkle with the remaining cheddar cheese. Bake 45–50 min or until a knife inserted near the center comes out clean. Let stand for 10 min before cutting.

YIELD: *6 servings*
COOK TIME:
45–55 min

INGREDIENTS:

7 eggs

5 egg yolks

1 cup heavy whipping cream

1 cup half and half

1 cup shredded mozzarella cheese

3/4 cup shredded sharp cheddar cheese

1/2 cup shredded Swiss cheese

2 tbsp finely chopped oil-packed sun dried tomatoes

$1\frac{1}{2}$ tsp salt-free seasoning blend

1/4 tsp dried basil

Lakeside Farm
13476 437th Ave
Webster, SD 57274
605-486-4430
gjhagen@venturecomm.net

Curried Eggs in Tomatoes

INGREDIENTS:

12 large ripe tomatoes (not Beefsteak, though)

12 large eggs

3/4 cup Parmesan cheese, freshly grated (optional)

FOR EACH TOMATO:

1 tsp white Worcestershire sauce

1 tsp dill

1 tsp chives (optional)

1 tsp thyme (optional)

1/4 tsp per tomato of curry

Whistling Swan Inn

110 Main St
Stanhope, NJ 07874
888-507-2337
info@whistlingswaninn.com
www.whistlingswaninn.com

INSTRUCTIONS:

Spray pan with non-stick cooking spray. Cut off the top of each tomato. If necessary, cut a very thin slice off bottom of each tomato to make a flat base so they won't flip over. Carefully scoop out enough pulp to leave room for each egg.

OPTION 1: Shake the 1 tsp of Worcestershire sauce and 1/4 tsp of curry into each tomato cup. Break an egg into each tomato cup. Sprinkle dill on top.

OPTION 2: Break an egg into tomato cup. Sprinkle each egg with 1 tbsp Parmesan cheese and each of herbs suggested above.

Bake in a 350F oven for 40 min, or until eggs have set but are not hard. Serve immediately.

YIELD: *12 servings*
COOK TIME: *40 min*

Ooey Gooey

INGREDIENTS:

- 4 large slices of bread

- 4 tbsp mayonnaise

- 8 eggs, fried

- 2 cups grated Vermont cheddar cheese

- 1 tsp paprika

Arlington's West Mountain Inn

144 West Mountain Inn Rd
Arlington, VT 05250
802-375-6516
info@westmountaininn.com
www.westmountaininn.com

INSTRUCTIONS:
Spread slices of bread with mayonnaise. Top each slice with 2 fried eggs and grated Vermont cheddar cheese. Melt under a broiler. Lightly sprinkle paprika on melted cheese to enhance flavor and add color.

YIELD: *4 servings*
COOK TIME: *10 min*

Egg Strudel with *Spinach Cream Sauce*

INGREDIENTS:

FOR EGG STRUDEL:

1 sheet frozen puff pastry, thawed

7 large eggs

3 tbsp whole milk

1/2 tsp salt

1/4 tsp black pepper

1/4 cup *each* chopped tomatoes and shredded Swiss cheese

FOR SPINACH CREAM SAUCE:

1 tbsp butter

1 cup frozen spinach

2 tbsp flour

1½ cups whole milk

1/4 tsp nutmeg

salt and pepper to taste

INSTRUCTIONS:

Whisk together 6 eggs, 2 tbsp milk, salt and pepper. Cook scrambled eggs in heated skillet. Make an egg wash by whisking one egg and 1 tbsp milk together in a bowl. Unroll the puff pastry sheet and lay out on counter with longest side facing you. Brush the top edge of pastry sheet with the egg wash. Place scrambled eggs 1/2 inch from the bottom of the puff pastry sheet. Sprinkle the tomatoes and Swiss cheese across the eggs.

Starting at the lower edge, roll pastry away from you, press the seam. Place seam side down on a parchment lined baking sheet. Brush top w/ egg wash and sprinkle lightly with salt. Bake at 375F for 20–30 min, until pastry is golden brown. Cut into 6 slices, giving two per serving. Top with heated spinach cream sauce.

To prepare sauce, melt butter in a non stick skillet. Add the frozen spinach and sauté until spinach is heated through and some of the water has evaporated. Sprinkle in the flour and stir for 2 min. Add milk and nutmeg. Cook over medium heat till sauce thickens. Season to taste with salt and pepper.

YIELD: *4 servings*
COOK TIME: *40 min*

The Inn & Spa at Intercourse Village

3542 Old Philadelphia Pike, Intercourse, PA 17534
717-768-2626
innkeeper@inn-spa.com
www.inn-spa.com

Rosemary & Goat Cheese Strata

NOTE: *Drizzle crème fraîche over individual casseroles, sprinkle a little paprika and top with a sprig of rosemary. Serve with bacon strips and broiled tomato. Original recipe from Gourmet 1997.*

INSTRUCTIONS:
Preheat oven to 350F.

In large bowl, tear or cut sliced bread into 1-inch pieces. Sprinkle chopped rosemary over bread cubes. Over this, crumble goat cheese. Mix gently with fingers or large slotted spoon. In medium bowl whisk together eggs, half and half, and spices. Pour egg mixture over bread mixture and combine well by gently mixing with large slotted spoon until egg soaks into bread cubes.

Divide mixture evenly among eight buttered 8-oz ramekins, filling 3/4 full. Put on baking sheet and into oven. Bake in middle of oven until puffed and golden, about 25–35 min. Cover with foil halfway through cooking if getting too brown. Remove from oven and let rest 5 min. Remove the stratas from the ramekins with a flexible spatula and place on plates.

YIELD: *8 servings*
COOK TIME: *25–35 min*

C.W. Worth House B&B
412 S 3rd St
Wilmington, NC 28401
800-340-8559
relax@worthhouse.com
www.worthhouse.com

INGREDIENTS:

1 loaf rustic bread such as ciabatta, sliced

1 tbsp fresh chopped rosemary

6-8 oz goat cheese, feta or a combination of cheeses to your liking

10 eggs

3 1/2 cups half and half

1/4 tsp cayenne

1/2 tsp dried thyme

Anne Hathaway's *CSA Strata*

INGREDIENTS:

FOR POLENTA:

1 cup corn meal

2 cup water, added slowly whisking

1 tsp salt

1/2 cup salsa

FOR FILLING:

To taste:

garlic

onion

zucchini

carrots

bell pepper

kale

chard

basil

parsley

eggplant

Parmesan

NOTE: *CSA stands for Community Supported Agriculture. We buy a share of a local farmer's produce for the season, in return for which we receive a box of fresh produce each week. The contents of the strata are dependent on what's in the box!*

INSTRUCTIONS:

POLENTA:
Cook cornmeal in salted water until it softly boils for 5 min, stirring all the time. Add 1/2 cup salsa, or any other spicy, tasty thing that's languishing in your fridge. Put in loaf pan overnight, covered with saran.

FILLING:
Sauté all fresh ingredients until pretty thoroughly cooked.

ASSEMBLY:
Slice polenta thinly and put on hot griddle until it acquires crust on both sides. Spray pie pan or 9-inch square pan lightly. Line with polenta slices. Place layer of filling. Sprinkle with Parmesan. Repeat process. Garnish top with pepper slices. Cook at 425F for about 25 min until golden brown.

YIELD: *6 servings*
COOK TIME: *25 min*

Anne Hathaway's Cottage
586 E Main St
Ashland, OR 97520
54-488-1050
innkeeper@ashlandbandb.com
www.ashlandbandb.com

Diva Tomato Basil Tart

INSTRUCTIONS:

Prepare tart shell. Combine flour and butter in food processor. Process to the fine crumb stage. Add one egg and process until dough forms a ball. Press evenly into bottom and sides of 9-inch spring form pan. Bake for 20 min in middle of oven. Crust will be firm to touch but not brown.

Thinly slice and lightly sprinkle tomatoes with kosher salt. Allow to drain in colander for 15 min or more. Place cheese in tart shell. Top with tomato slices and sprinkle with chives and basil.

Wisk together 3 eggs, half and half, mustard, salt and pepper and baking powder. Pour into shell. Bake at 350F for 25 to 35 min, until custard is firm (time depends on the variation in moisture in the cheese and tomatoes and the size of the eggs.) Allow to cool for 10 min.

YIELD: *6 servings*
COOK TIME: *25–35 min*

INGREDIENTS:

1½ cup flour

1/2 cup cold butter, cubed

4 large eggs

1 cup grated mozzarella

4 Roma tomatoes

2 tbsp fresh chives, minced

1/4 cup fresh basil leaves

3/4 cup half and half

1/2 tsp ground mustard, optional

1/4 tsp salt

1/4 tsp black pepper

pinch of baking powder

Morgan Hill Retreat
1921 Northeast Sawdust Hill Rd
Poulsbo, WA 98370
360-598-4930
marcia@morganhillretreat.com
www.morganhillretreat.com

Vegetable Omelet in *Puff Pastry*

INGREDIENTS:

puff pastry dough

5 eggs

1 cup heavy cream

1/4 cup onions, chopped

1/2 cup spinach, chopped

1/3 cup *each* red bell peppers and zucchini, chopped

1/8 cup ricotta cheese

3 egg yolks

juice of 1/2 lemon

1/4 tsp salt

2 dashes white pepper

1 dash cayenne pepper

1/2 lb unsalted butter

Carter House Inns

301 L St
Eureka, CA 95501
800-404-1390
reserve@carterhouse.com
www.carterhouse.com

INSTRUCTIONS:

Preheat oven to 350F.

Lightly grease a large tart pan. Take a circular cut-out of pastry dough and lay it on the bottom of the pan so that it conforms to the pan and reaches up the sides.

Whip together eggs and cream. Top the dough with egg/cream mixture. Add onions, spinach, peppers, zucchini, and cheese. Place another layer of puff pastry over the top of these ingredients and form a pouch around the filling. Bake for 30 min.

In a double boiler, make hollandaise sauce by whipping egg yolks and lemon juice until the mixture has a custard-like consistency. Add salt and both peppers. In a separate pan, melt butter and add it slowly to the mixture, whipping constantly.

When the pastry is removed from the oven, cover it with hollandaise sauce and serve.

YIELD: *10 servings*
COOK TIME: *30 min*

Corn & Cheese Flan

Above: breakfast at Colonial Pines Inn B&B

INGREDIENTS:

8 oz grated white cheddar cheese

8 oz frozen corn

9 eggs

1/2 tsp salt

1/2 tsp pepper

1/4 tsp nutmeg

1/8 tsp cayenne

3/4 cup skim milk

3/4 cup half and half

2 tbsp grated Parmesan

INSTRUCTIONS:

Preheat oven to 325F. Spray a half size commercial pan or a 9x13-inch pan with cooking spray. Layer cheese and corn twice. Mix up all remaining ingredients except Parmesan and pour over.

Bake 45–55 min until puffy & lightly browned. Sprinkle with Parmesan. Loosen carefully from sides, cut into rectangles and serve.

YIELD: *6 servings*
COOK TIME: *45–55 min*

Colonial Pines Inn B&B

541 Hickory St

Highlands, NC 28741

866-526-2060

sleeptight@colonialpinesinn.com

www.colonialpinesinn.com

Montana Potato Pie

INGREDIENTS:

3 lbs Jimmy Dean Hot Breakfast Sausage

1 cup chopped onions

1 cup chopped peppers

1 pkg O'Brian Potatoes (frozen) Orida brand

1½ eggs for each baking bowl

FOR EVERY 6 TO 7 SERVINGS:

1 cup cottage cheese

1/2 cup grated Parmesan cheese

1/2 cup grated sharp cheddar cheese

1/2 cup sour cream

1 tsp salt

1 tsp pepper

INSTRUCTIONS:

Cook sausage in heavy large skillet over medium-high heat until brown, breaking into small pieces with back of spoon, about 5 min. Mix in onions, peppers and cook until onions turn clear (3 to 5 min). Mix in potatoes, cover and cook about 5 more min until potatoes are soft. Turn off heat and let stand covered until cool if preparing for refrigeration. Spray small baking bowls with non-stick spray. Pour about 1/2 cup of mixture into baking bowls. Prepare up to 48 hrs ahead and refrigerate. Mix can be prepared up to 2 weeks ahead and frozen.

In a large mixing bowl, mix eggs and other in-gredients together. Pour 1/2 cup plus into each prepared baking bowl.

Preheat oven to 350F. Bake for 30 to 35 min until tops start to brown slightly. Sprinkle with paprika and serve hot.

YIELD: *6–7 servings*
COOK TIME: *45–50 min*

Bad Rock B&B
480 Bad Rock Dr
Columbia Falls, MT 59912
406-892-2829
Stay@badrock.com
www.badrock.com

Stuffed Monkeys

NOTE: *Folklore has it that this Dutch pastry was called Stuffed Monninkendammers, but when it was brought over to England from Holland and the name proved to be too much of a mouthful, these tasty tea-time treats were dubbed Stuffed Monkeys!*

INSTRUCTIONS:

Prepare Vinegar Pastry the night before. Mix all ingredients together. Dough will be wet, use spatula to scrape from sides and transfer to wax paper. Wrap in wax paper and wrap again in foil paper. Put in refrigerator overnight.

STUFFED MONKEYS: Roll out vinegar pastry using liberal flour on rolling surface and rolling pin to avoid sticking, and cut into rectangular shape about 7x11 inches. Spread strawberry jam down middle of pastry about 2 inches wide (1 large spoonful for each stuffed monkey). Chop dried fruit and spread 3–4 tbsp of mixture on top of jam. Sprinkle with 1/2 tsp cinnamon and 1/2 tsp sugar. Close up pastry. Turn the stuffed monkey over. Brush with egg. Indent with knife at regular intervals. Sprinkle with sugar.

Bake on flat, ungreased baking tray at 375F for about 20–25 min. Don't let them get too dark.

Remove from oven and cut each stuffed monkey in half to transfer to cooling rack (to avoid breaking pastry). When cooled, cut into half-inch strips. Sprinkle with confectioner's sugar and serve with tea.

YIELD: *55 servings*
COOK TIME: *20–25 min*

INGREDIENTS:

VINEGAR PASTRY:

1 lb all purpose flour (3¾ cups)

3 sticks margarine (not butter)

2 tbsp malt vinegar

3 tbsp cold water

2 egg yolks

3 tbsp sugar

FILLING:

strawberry jam

1/4 cup *each* light and dark raisins

1/2 cup *each* dried apricots and dates

cinnamon to sprinkle

sugar to sprinkle

1 egg, beaten

confectioner's sugar for garnish

Channel Bass Inn
6228 Church St
Chincoteague, VA 23336
800-249-0818
barbara@channelbassinn.com
www.channelbassinn.com

Dinsmore House Torta Rustica

INGREDIENTS:

1 lb puff pastry

12 large eggs

Boursin cheese (1/2 to 3/4 container)

3 tbsp butter

10 oz Swiss cheese, thinly sliced

spinach

8 oz smoked ham, thinly sliced

6 large roasted red bell peppers

egg wash (1 large egg beaten with 1 tbsp water and a pinch of salt)

INSTRUCTIONS:

Preheat oven to 425F.

To prepare crust, generously butter a 9-inch springform pan. Cut off 1/4 of puff pastry and set aside. Roll out remaining puff pastry to 1/4 inch thick, place in bottom of the pan, leaving 1-inch overhang. Cover with plastic wrap and refrigerate.

Roll out the smaller piece of pastry until it is 1/4 inch thick. Cut out a 9-inch circle of dough to place on top of the torta and place it aside. Cover with plastic wrap and refrigerate.

To prepare filling, whisk eggs, boursin cheese, salt and pepper to taste in a large bowl. Melt butter in large skillet over low heat and pour in egg mixture. Gently but constantly stir eggs until cooked. Eggs should be scrambled slowly and loosely.

Place cooked eggs aside and let cool.

Retrieve spring form pan from refrigerator and layer the ingredients in the following order: 1/4 of swiss cheese, half the eggs, half the spinach, 1/4 the cheese, half the ham, all the roasted red peppers (laid out flat). Continue layering in the reverse order with the remaining ham, 1/4 the cheese, spinach, eggs, and 1/4 the cheese. Make sure to spread the ingredients all the way to the edge of the pan.

Fold the excess pastry over the top of the filling and brush the edge of the crust you've created with egg wash. Retrieve the smaller pastry circle from the refrigerator and place over the top of the filling. Gently push the top crust down the sides of the pan, pressing and sealing the top crust to the bottom crust. Brush with egg wash. Cut a small hole in the top of the crust to vent. Bake about 1 hr, or until crust is puffed and golden brown.

YIELD: *10 servings*
COOK TIME: *1 hr*

Dinsmore House Inn
1211 W Main St
Charlottesville, VA 22903
877-882-7829
info@dinsmorehouse.com
www.dinsmorehouse.com

Starters
and Sides

WHETHER YOU'RE LOOKING TO compliment wines, cheeses, or the main entrée, the following pages are filled with recipes sure to energize and invigorate the taste buds. From appetizers, hors d'oeuvres, side dishes, soups, salads, and even some refreshing beverages, these recipes will please your every mood and appetite.

Thick and hearty soups as well as wholesome broths are wonderful on a chilly day, but soups can also be enjoyed during the hottest summer months. Try a chilled soup such as the tangy *Moroccan-Spiced Cold Tomato Soup* from Artist's Inn & Gallery or the sweet and creamy *Boreas Berry Fruit Soup* from Boreas B&B Inn.

Vegetables are an important part of a healthy lifestyle, and it's never been easier to incorporate them into our diet than with these colorful salads of fresh veggies and fruits and healthy home-made vinaigrettes from America's bed and break-fasts, inns and guesthouses.

Side dishes enhance any meal. Transform mushrooms with the English Rose Inn's recipe for *Devonshire Mushrooms*. Liven up your favorite grilled meats with *Rick's Bourbon Onions* from Fairville Inn. These winning starters and sides will keep your dinner guests coming back for more!

The appetite is sharpened by the first bites.

JOSE RIZAL

Minted Raspberry Cooler

INGREDIENTS:

1/2 cup fresh mint leaves, plus mint sprigs for garnish

1 cup boiling water

1 6-oz can frozen lemonade concentrate

1 pint fresh raspberries crushed and sweetened with 1/2 cup sugar (or 1 10-oz pkg frozen raspberries)

crushed ice

2 cups cold water

INSTRUCTIONS:

Combine 1/2 cup mint leaves and boiling water. Let steep 5 min. Add raspberries and frozen lemonade concentrate. Stir (until thawed, if frozen raspberries are used). Strain into pitcher half-filled with crushed ice. Add cold water and stir. Garnish with fresh mint leaves.

YIELD: *8 servings*

Bishopsgate Inn
7 Norwich Rd
East Haddam, CT 06423
860-873-1677
ctkagel@bishopsgate.com
www.bishopsgate.com

Wassail for All Ages!

NOTE: *This soothing beverage is traditionally served during the holidays and is delightful served either warm or cold.*

INSTRUCTIONS:
Combine all ingredients in sauce pan. Bring to a boil and simmer for 5 to 10 min. Serve warm or cold.

YIELD: *3½ quarts*
COOK TIME: *5–10 min*

INGREDIENTS:

1½ quarts unsweetened orange juice

1 quart apple juice

1/3 cup light corn syrup

6 sticks cinnamon

24 whole cloves

1 lemon sliced for garnish, optional

Woody Hill B&B
149 S Woody Hill Rd
Westerly, RI 02891
401-322-0452
woodyhillbandb@verizon.net
www.woodyhill.com

DOBSON HOUSE

Cindy & Ted's Salsaah!

INGREDIENTS:

1 lb cream cheese (low fat can be used)

1/2 bunch fresh cilantro

1 clove garlic (don't be tempted to use more)

prepared salsa to taste

Dobson House
PO Box 1584
El Prado, NM 87529
575-776-5738
dobhouse@newmex.com
www.new-mexico-bed-and-breakfast.com

INSTRUCTIONS:
Cut cream cheese into chunks. Trim long stems from cilantro. Put all ingredients in a food processor and blend until smooth. Serve chilied with chunks of French bread, bagel chips, fresh vegetables or Jicama.

YIELD: *16 servings*

Jalapeño Cilantro Hummus

NOTE: *Hummus is such an easy appetizer or sandwich spread, keeps well and can be so versatile. During the summer months when my jalapeños are so abundant and the cilantro is growing like a weed, this is a great mix!*

INSTRUCTIONS:
Blend all ingredients in food processor. Use the leftover juice from the chickpeas to get the right consistency. I use about 3/4 cup. Tastes even better day 2 after flavors had time to meld.

Enjoy with Pita chips or on a sandwich.

YIELD: *16 servings*

INGREDIENTS:

2 cans chickpeas, drained and rinsed, but WAIT! Save some of the juice for later...

3 tbsp fresh lime juice

3/4 cup cilantro (rough chop)

3 jalapeños, seeded and rough chopped —you may adjust numbers here based on your spice tolerance

3 cloves of garlic peeled and smashed, rough chop

3 tbsp tahini

Salt to taste (1/4–1/2 tsp)

Whispering Pines B&B
2018 6th Ave
Nebraska City, NE 68410
402-873-5850
innkeeper@bbwhispering-pines.com
www.bbwhisperingpines.com

JIFFY

Olive Tuscan Bread

INGREDIENTS:

1 1/2 cups "JIFFY" Baking Mix

1/2 tsp Italian herbs or herbs de Provence

1/4 tsp garlic powder

dash of pepper

1/3 cup finely grated Parmesan cheese

1 cup milk

1/4 cup olive oil

1 egg

20–24 pitted olives

grated cheese & paprika (optional)

INSTRUCTIONS:
Preheat oven to 375F.

Oil a 9x13-inch pan/dish.

Mix dry ingredients including the cheese. Add milk, olive oil, and egg. Pour into prepared pan/dish. Let sit for 5 min.

Poke olives into batter in rows with about 1 1/2 inches between rows.

Bake for 20 min. When out of the oven, brush with olive oil. For a bit of added color, sprinkle your favorite grated cheese on top of bread and add a sprinkle of paprika, or reserve a pinch of herbs and sprinkle on top.

YIELD: *10–12 servings*
COOK TIME: *20 min*

Mexican Confetti Muffins

INSTRUCTIONS:
Sauté red pepper, green onions, and corn together in 2 tbsp of butter for 10 min. Remove from heat. Drain and add green chilies. Continue to cool while preparing the batter. Mix corn muffin mix, egg, milk, cheese, and Tabasco sauce together until smooth. Add cooled veggies to batter and blend. Spoon mixture into muffin pan (greased or with liners). Cook at 400F for 25 min or until golden brown.

YIELD: *1 dozen small muffins*
COOK TIME: *35 min*

AND ANOTHER FAVORITE FROM JIFFY...

Hot Diggity Dog Corn Muffins

2 boxes "JIFFY" Corn Muffin mix
2/3 cup milk
2 eggs
1 tsp dry mustard
1/2 tsp paprika
4 hot dogs, chopped into small pieces
1/3 cup ketchup

Preheat oven to 400F. Mix together muffin mix, milk, eggs, and spices. Place 1 spoonful of the batter into each muffin cup. Mix together the hot dog pieces and the ketchup. Distribute the hot dog mixture evenly into the muffin cups. Top with the remaining batter. Bake for 20 min.

YIELD: *2 dozen*
COOK TIME: *20 min*

INGREDIENTS:

1/2 cup red pepper, finely diced

2 green onions, chopped

1/3 cup of frozen corn

1 small can of green chilies

1 pkg "JIFFY" Corn Muffin Mix

1 egg

1/2 cup milk

3/4 cup grated cheddar cheese

1/8 tsp Tabasco sauce

Moroccan-Spiced Cold Tomato Soup

INGREDIENTS:

1 small onion, chopped

2 tbsp olive oil

1 tsp paprika

1/4 tsp *each* ground ginger, ground cumin, and ground cinnamon

4 large fresh tomatoes, peeled and seeded

1³/₄ cups chicken broth

2 tsp honey

2 tbsp *each* fresh parsley and cilantro, chopped

1 tsp fresh lemon juice

Sour cream for garnish

Artist's Inn & Gallery

117 E Main St
Terre Hill, PA 17581
888-999-4479
stay@artistinn.com
www.artistinn.com

INSTRUCTIONS:

Cook onion in oil with spices in a 3-quart heavy saucepan over moderate heat, stirring occasionally, until onion is softened and begins to brown, 4 to 5 min. Coarsely chop tomatoes and add to onion mixture with broth and honey. Bring to a boil. Transfer soup to metal bowl set in a larger bowl of ice and cold water. Add cilantro, lemon juice and parsley. Cool soup, stirring occasionally until cold, 15 to 20 min. Add salt and pepper to taste and serve with a dollop of sour cream.

YIELD: *4 servings*

Harvest Day Soup

INGREDIENTS:

- 1 lb sausage
- 1 onion, finely chopped
- 2½ cups chicken broth
- 2 cups cooked pumpkin
- 1 tsp lemon juice
- 2 cups hot milk
- 1/2 tsp nutmeg
- 1/4 tsp cinnamon
- salt & pepper to taste
- chopped parsley

INSTRUCTIONS:

In large frying pan brown and crumble sausage. Remove sausage and sauté onions in drippings. Transfer onions and sausage to crock pot and add remaining ingredients, except parsley.

Heat to a simmer. Sprinkle with parsley and serve warm.

YIELD: *8–10 servings*
COOK TIME: *2 hrs*

1851 Historic Maple Hill Manor B&B

2941 Perryville Rd
Springfield, KY 40069
859-336-3075
maplehillmanorbb@aol.com
www.maplehillmanor.com

Chilled Greek Cucumber Avocado Soup

INGREDIENTS:

3 English cucumbers

1 Spanish or Vidalia onion

4 garlic cloves, minced

2 avocados, chopped

kosher salt and freshly ground pepper to taste

1/4 cup *each* mint, cilantro, and Italian parsley, chopped

1/4 cup chives, snipped

2 tsp *each* dried oregano and dried dillweed

1 cup feta, crumbled

1 tbsp harissa or chili paste

16 oz plain yogurt

1/2–3/4 cup sour cream

1 cup lemon juice

1/2 cup extra virgin olive oil

INSTRUCTIONS:

Peel, seed and chop the cucumbers. Dice onions and dice, mince, or chop remaining vegetables and herbs, as noted.

Combine all the ingredients in a large bowl. Blend using an immersion blender until creamy and well combined. Adjust seasoning to taste. Serve with queso fresco or fresh goat cheese.

YIELD: *8 servings*

Chestnut Street Inn
301 E Chestnut St
Sheffield, IL 61361
800-537-1304
monikaandjeff@chestnut-inn.com
www.chestnut-inn.com

Boreas Berry Fruit Soup

NOTE: *This dish is a beautiful deep, dark pink-red in color and the taste is rich and full of luscious berries (an excellent source of antioxidants!). Since one of the bounties of the Long Beach, Washington Peninsula is the cranberry, we use them frequently.*

INSTRUCTIONS:
In a 3-quart saucepan, bring cranberries (fresh or frozen) and apple juice to a boil. Reduce heat and simmer uncovered for 10 min. Add raspberries and boil for a min or so. Press through a sieve or run through a food mill to remove seeds, and return the juice to pan. Bring to a boil. Add sugar, lemon or lime juice and cinnamon and remove from heat. Cool for 5 min and then stir 1 cup of soup mixture into 1½ cups cream. Return all to pan and bring to a gentle boil. Mix cornstarch with remaining cream; stir into soup. Cook and stir for 2 min (don't allow rolling boil).

Pour into bowl sitting over ice bath until room temperature. Then chill in refrigerator. Serve chilled. Garnish with whipped cream, fresh berries and mint.

YIELD: *6 servings*
COOK TIME:
25 min

INGREDIENTS:

2 cups cranberries

2 cups apple juice

1 cup unsweetened raspberries or any other berries

1/2–1 cup sugar to taste

1 tbsp fresh lemon juice

1/2 tsp ground cinnamon

2 cups half and half, divided

1 tbsp cornstarch

whipped cream for garnish

Boreas B&B Inn
607 N Ocean Beach Blvd
Long Beach, WA 98631
888-642-8069
info@boreasinn.com
www.boreasinn.com

Bisque of Roasted Vegetables

INGREDIENTS:

2 zucchinis

2 large yellow squash

2 carrots

4 large tomatoes

2 medium onions

1 butternut squash

olive oil, salt, sugar, pepper (to taste)

2 tbsp balsamic vinegar

1 pint heavy cream

INSTRUCTIONS:

Preheat oven to 350F.

Slice zucchini and yellow squash. Peel and slice carrots. Slice tomatoes and onions in half. Peel and dice butternut squash.

Combine vegetables in a roasting pan. Rub with olive oil, salt, pepper, and sugar. Bake in 350F oven until nice caramelization develops on the edges of the vegetables.

Transfer the vegetables to a stockpot and add water to the level of the vegetables. Simmer until all are very tender. Purée with either a food processor or blender. Strain.

Season with salt, pepper, sugar and balsamic vinegar. Finish with heavy cream.

YIELD: *15 portions*
COOK TIME: *1 hour*

Inn at Pleasant Lake
853 Pleasant St
New London, NH 03257
603-526-6271
info@innatpleasantlake.com
www.innatpleasantlake.com

French Onion Soup with *Three Cheeses*

INSTRUCTIONS:

Melt the butter in a heavy 4-quart sauce pan. Add onions and sauté over low heat until soft. Sprinkle in flour and stir. Pour in the stock. Season with salt and pepper. Cover and cook over low heat for 45 min. Stir occasionally.

Divide soup into 8 flameproof bowls. Place 2 slices of toasted bread on top of each bowl.

Mix cheeses together in bowl. Sprinkle soup with cheeses. Place bowls under broiler until cheese is melted and browned. Serve immediately.

YIELD: *8 servings*
COOK TIME: *45 min*

INGREDIENTS:

3 oz unsalted butter

1 lb yellow onions, thinly sliced

1 tbsp all-purpose flour

1½ quarts chicken stock

salt

freshly ground black pepper

16 slices French baguette, toasted

3 oz Swiss cheese grated

3 oz Provolone cheese grated

3 oz Emmental cheese grated

Golden Pheasant Inn

763 River Rd
Erwinna, PA 18920
800-830-4474
barbara@goldenpheasant.com
www.goldenpheasant.com

Chicken-Apple-Nut Salad

INGREDIENTS:

2 cups boneless, skinless chicken breast

1 tbsp olive oil

1/2 cup mayonnaise

4 tbsp honey

3 tbsp Dijon mustard

pinch of rosemary

2 cups diced apples (red or green, about 5 medium)

1/2 cup chopped walnuts

1/2 cup chopped celery

2 large red lettuce leaves

1870 Wedgwood Bed & Breakfast Inn of New Hope, PA
111 W Bridge St
New Hope, PA 18938
215-862-2570
stay@wedgwoodinn.com
www.WedgwoodInn.com

INSTRUCTIONS:
Dice chicken and cook in 1 tbsp olive oil in a skillet. Let cool. While chicken cools, combine the mayonnaise, honey, mustard, and rosemary in a small bowl. In a big bowl, combine cooled chicken, apples, walnuts, and celery. Fold the mayonnaise mixture into the chicken mixture and chill for 1 hr.

Serve chilled over a red lettuce leaf.

YIELD: *2 servings*

Strawberry Spinach Salad

FOR SALAD:

2 bunches fresh spinach, cleaned and broken into pieces

1½ pint of strawberries, sliced

FOR DRESSING:

3/4 cup corn oil

1/3 cup fresh lemon juice

1/2 cup of sugar

1 onion, peeled and chopped

1 tsp salt

1 tsp dried mustard

1/2 tsp lemon peel

1 tbsp poppy seeds

INSTRUCTIONS:
Mix the dressing ingredients together and chill until ready to serve. Pour over spinach and strawberries and toss.

YIELD: *8 servings*

Lamplight Inn B&B
231 Lake Ave
Lake Luzerne, NY 12846
800-262-4668
stay@lamplightinn.com
www.lamplightinn.com

Endive Salad with Walnuts

INGREDIENTS:

6 tbsp olive oil

2 tbsp minced green onion

2 tsp Dijon mustard

1/2 tsp sugar

1 Granny Smith apple, peeled, cored, and sliced

6 large Belgian endive, separate leaves (wipe, don't wash!)

2–3 lbs coarsely chopped walnuts

2–3 lbs finely cubed Roquefort cheese

freshly ground pepper

NOTE: *The leaves of Belgian endive are shaped like small, oblong scoops and are ideal for holding a bite of something as savory and scrumptious as this fruit, cheese and nut mixture.*

INSTRUCTIONS:

Combine oil, onion, mustard, sugar and apple in a salad bowl and whisk until thoroughly blended. Place the endive leaves into the bowl, then sprinkle with walnuts, cheese and pepper to taste. Chill. Just before serving, toss the salad. Arrange the leaves on a platter or plate and then "load" them with the mixture.

YIELD: *4 servings*

**Yelton Manor B&B
& The Manor
Guest House**
140 North Shore Dr
South Haven, MI 49090
269-637-5220
elaine@yeltonmanor.com
www.yeltonmanor.com

Wilted Spinach Salad

Eagle Harbor Inn
9914 Water St
Ephraim, WI 54211
800-324-5427
nedd@eagleharbor.com
www.EagleHarborInn.com

INSTRUCTIONS:

Stir vinegar, sugar, pepper & salt together in small bowl until sugar dissolves. Cut bacon into 1/2-inch pieces and fry. Reserve rendered fat.

Use 3 tbsp of bacon fat to sauté onion and garlic, about 3 min, until just translucent. Add vinegar mixture for 1 min then remove from stove. Working quickly scrape bottom of skillet with wooden spoon to get browned bits also.

Wash spinach and put in large bowl. Pour dressing over spinach, add bacon, and toss gently with tongs until spinach is slightly wilted.

Peel hardboiled eggs and cut lengthwise into quarters. Arrange eggs on top.

YIELD: *4 servings*

INGREDIENTS:

3 tbsp cider vinegar

1 tbsp sugar

1/2 tsp pepper

pinch salt

8 slices bacon

1/2 med red onion, medium chopped

1 small garlic clove, minced

6 oz spinach

3 large eggs, hardboiled

Nutty Chicken Salad

INGREDIENTS:

4–5 chicken breasts

2 cups halved grapes

1/2 cup chopped pecans

juice of 1 lemon

1/2 cup maple syrup

1 1/2 cup mayonnaise

chives to taste

Inn at Herr Ridge

900 Chambersburg Rd
Gettysburg, PA 17235
800-362-9849
info@herrtavern.com
www.herrtavern.com

INSTRUCTIONS:

Grill chicken breasts. Allow to cool and dice into large pieces. Mix grapes, pecans, lemon juice, maple syrup, and mayo in a bowl. Fold in chicken and chives. Serve with grilled pineapple rings, and an oil and vinegar salad.

YIELD: *2 quarts*

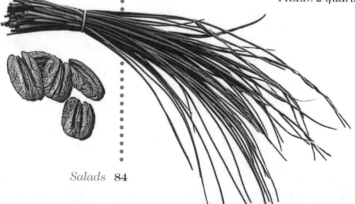

Mesclun Greens with *Sherry-Walnut Vinaigrette*

INSTRUCTIONS:
Combine first 7 ingredients in processor and blend until combined. Toss with salad greens, grapes, and blue cheese.

Makes 3/4 cup vinaigrette to serve 6–8 main salads.

YIELD: *6–8 servings*

INGREDIENTS:

1/4 cup sherry vinegar

2 tbsp shallots, minced

2 tbsp honey

1/2 tsp Dijon mustard

salt & pepper

2 tbsp extra virgin olive oil

2 tbsp walnut oil

salad greens— your choice

1/2 cup walnuts

1 cup halved red grapes

1/2 cup blue cheese crumbles

Christopher Place
1500 Pinnacles Way
Newport, TN 37821
423-623-6555
marston@christopherplace.com
www.christopherplace.com

Fried Rice with a Kick!

Mistletoe Bough
497 Hillabee St
Alexander City, AL 35010
256-329-3717
mistletoebough@charter.net
www.mistletoebough.com

INGREDIENTS:

2 tbsp hot sesame oil (chili sesame)

2 tbsp canola or peanut oil

3 cups cooked rice

2 green onions, chopped

2 tbsp soy sauce

1/2 cup chopped almonds

1 cup frozen mixed vegetables, thawed (or fresh veggies of your choice)

2 eggs, beaten

INSTRUCTIONS:

Heat oils in large skillet or wok. Add rice, green onion, soy sauce, almonds, and vegetables stirring to mix. Add egg and continue to stir. Fry until desired consistency.

YIELD: *6 servings*

Minnesota Wild Rice Patties

NOTE: *Makes 4 burger size patties. I make the patties smaller for a nice "sausage-like" side.*

INSTRUCTIONS:
Combine the wild rice with the cheese and eggs. Stir in 1/3 cup cracker crumbs, salt, pepper, and herbs if desired. Mix well and shape into patties.

Dip both sides of the patties in the remaining 1/3 cup cracker crumbs and brown on both sides in a small amount of oil in a skillet on medium high heat (best to pre-heat the skillet).

YIELD: *4 servings*
COOK TIME: *3–5 min*

INGREDIENTS:

2 cups cooked wild rice

1/2 cup grated sharp cheddar cheese, and/or smoked Gouda, Havarti, Swiss, Muenster, etc.

2 eggs, lightly beaten

2/3 cup fine, dry cracker crumbs and/or seasoned bread crumbs

1 tsp salt

dash pepper

Herbes de Provence, ground sage, and thyme, all optional

vegetable or olive oil

A.G. Thomson House

2617 E Third St
Duluth, MN 55812
877-807-8077
info@thomsonhouse.biz
www.thomsonhouse.biz

FAIRVILLE INN

Rick's Bourbon Onions

INGREDIENTS:

4–5 medium onions, yellow or sweet

4 tbsp butter

1 tbsp sugar

1/2 – 3/4 cup stock/broth (beef, chicken, or vegetable)

1/2 cup bourbon, or more to taste

freshly ground pepper to taste

Fairville Inn
506 Kennett Pike, Rt 52
Chadds Ford, PA 19317
877-285-7772
info@fairvilleinn.com
www.fairvilleinn.com

NOTE: *We invariably get recipe requests when we serve these onions as a topping to omelets. These are also especially good on grilled chicken breasts, hamburgers, steaks, and grilled tuna or swordfish steaks.*

INSTRUCTIONS:
Trim off tops and bottoms of the onions, cut them in half length-wise, and remove skins. Place flat side down on a cutting board, and slice cross-wise into half-rings about 3/8-inch thick. Separate the rings as best you can. Melt the butter over medium-low heat in a 12-inch skillet. Add the onion rings and cook very slowly, stirring frequently, until the onions begin to soften and get limp. This takes time, but don't be tempted to increase the heat too much—you don't want to brown the onions at this point. When the onions are softened, sprinkle in the sugar and stir well. Raise the heat to medium-high (no more) and continue to cook the onions, stirring a bit more frequently, until they become a nice medium golden brown. Again, this takes time, but it is well worth it.

Reduce the heat to medium, add the stock and continue cooking until it is almost evaporated. Add the bourbon and freshly ground pepper to taste, and cook until almost all the liquid has evaporated. Add a final splash (or two) of bourbon and stir. Check to see if it needs a touch of salt if you did not use a high-sodium stock or broth.

YIELD: *2 cups*
COOK TIME: *45 min*

Traditional Potato Salad

INSTRUCTIONS:
Put potatoes in large saucepan and cover with cold water. Bring to a boil and cook for 20-30 min, until potatoes are tender but still firm. Drain the potatoes and let cool slightly. Cut into 1/2-inch pieces.

Put the potatoes in large bowl and add parsley, dill, scallions, celery, vinegar, and mayonnaise. Season to taste with salt and black pepper; toss gently to mix. Cover and chill until the flavors have had time to blend.

YIELD: *6 servings*
COOK TIME: *20–30 min*

INGREDIENTS:

1¹/₂ lbs red potatoes (about 5 medium potatoes)

2 tbsp chopped parsley

2 tbsp chopped fresh dill or 3/4 tsp dried

2 scallions, trimmed and finely chopped

1/2 stalk of celery, chopped

2 tbsp vinegar

1 cup mayonnaise

salt

freshly ground black pepper

Dockside Guest Quarters

22 Harris Island Rd
York, ME 03909
888-860-7428
eric@docksidegq.com
www.docksidegq.com

Devonshire Mushrooms

INGREDIENTS:

8 oz white button mushrooms

1 clove garlic, crushed

2 tbsp onion, finely chopped

1 tbsp butter

2 tbsp white wine

4 tbsp sour cream

2 tbsp fresh parsley, chopped

INSTRUCTIONS:

In a sauté pan add the mushrooms, garlic, onion and butter. Stir and cook on medium heat for 5 min, add white wine and cook for 5 more min. Remove the pan from the heat and stir in the sour cream and parsley. Serve immediately.

YIELD: *2 servings*
COOK TIME: *10 min*

English Rose Inn
195 Vermont Rt 242
Montgomery Center, VT 05471
888-303-3232
englishroseinn@fairpoint.net
www.englishroseinnvermont.com

Summer Squash

INSTRUCTIONS:

Slice squash into coins and remove large seeds. Place squash in large frying pan. Top with sliced onion. Add water, salt, and pepper. Cook over medium heat with lid on pan. Stir a few times to prevent sticking. When squash is "fork tender," add butter and brown sugar. Do not overcook.

YIELD: *6 servings*
COOK TIME: *20 min*

INGREDIENTS:

4–5 medium-size yellow squash

1 tbsp onion, sliced

1/2 cup water

1 tsp salt

1 tsp pepper

2 tbsp butter

2 tbsp light brown sugar

Hickory Bridge Farm
96 Hickory Bridge Rd
Orrtanna, PA 17353
717-642-5261
info@hickorybridgefarm.com
www.hickorybridgefarm.com

Main
Entrées

THERE ARE MANY THINGS IN LIFE such as family and work that keep us "on-the-go" and make it easy to fall back to the same old dishes over and over again. When it comes time to treat your palate to a sensational meal, browse the following pages and you'll find yourself immersed in a broad selection of dinner entrées ranging from the oh-so-simple but never boring *Change-Up Chicken* to the elaborate guest-worthy *Grilled Beef Tenderloin with Red Wine & Pistachios*. You can cook up family-favorite comfort foods in a jiffy, like *Chicken Pot Pie* or *Tamale Pie*, or dazzle guests with elegant *Pesto and Lemon Chicken Linguine* from the White Oak Inn. And regional specialties like the Fairview Inn's *Mouthwatering Mississippi Crab Cakes* will help kick it up a notch in the kitchen!

Your entrée will be the heart and soul of your meal, so making it special, unique, comforting and delicious will bring satisfaction to your dinner guests and exceed their expectations. Your main entrée will be the crowning achievement of a truly exquisite meal, a signature dish that will impress and enchant for many nights to come.

A man seldom thinks with more earnestness of anything than he does of his dinner.

SAMUEL JOHNSON

Nuttin' Like Chicken-n-Stuffin' *Casserole*

CORN BREAD:

1 pkg "JIFFY" Corn Muffin Mix

1 egg

1/3 cup + 1 tbsp milk

FILLING:

1 can condensed cream of mushroom or celery soup

1¼ cups milk

4 medium green onions, chopped

1 cup frozen peas or frozen mixed vegetables

2 cups of cooked turkey or chicken in bite-sized cubes

1/2 tsp salt

pepper

STUFFING:

1 small chopped onion

1 cup diced celery

1/8 tsp salt

1/2 tsp sage

1 tsp parsley flakes

1/4 cup butter (1/2 stick), melted

1 egg

1 cup of chicken broth

INSTRUCTIONS:

Preheat oven to 400F and grease an 8-inch square pan or a 9x13-inch pan.

First, bake the corn bread for the stuffing: Blend corn muffin mix, 1 egg and milk. Pour into 8-inch square pan and cook for 20 min. When done, set aside and let cool.

Lower the oven temperature to 350F. In a saucepan heat the soup and milk. Bring to a boil stirring frequently. Add the green onion, frozen peas/vegetables and return to a boil. Remove from heat and stir in the meat, salt, and pepper. Pour filling into prepared baking dish.

For the stuffing, stir the onion, celery, salt, sage and parsley. Add the melted butter and continue stirring. Crumble the corn bread into the vegetable mixture. Add the egg and chicken broth. Spoon the stuffing on top of the meat and gently spread it evenly on top.

Cover the casserole and cook for 30 min. Take off the cover and continue cooking for 30 min.

YIELD: *4–6 servings*
COOK TIME: *1 hr 20 min*

Pesto and Lemon Chicken Linguine

INSTRUCTIONS:

Bring water for pasta to a boil.

Cut chicken into bite size pieces and sauté in olive oil for 5 or 6 min. Remove from skillet and set aside.

Wash mushrooms and cut in half. Add 2 tbsp of butter to skillet and sauté mushroom halves. Remove from skillet and set aside.

Add pasta to boiling water and start a timer for 9 min.

Melt remaining 3 tbsp of butter and whisk in flour to make a roux. Cook over medium heat for 1 min. Gradually whisk in chicken stock. Add wine, lemon juice and lemon rind. Return chicken and mushrooms to the pan.

When timer goes off, put the asparagus (cut into 1½ inch pieces) in the pan with the pasta and cook for 3 to 4 min longer. Stir the pesto into the sauce. Drain pasta and toss with sauce. Serve with grated cheese on top.

YIELD: *8 servings*
COOK TIME: *20–25 min*

INGREDIENTS:

About 1 lb linguine pasta

8 boneless skinless chicken breasts

2 8-oz pkgs mushrooms

2 tbsp + 3 tbsp butter

2 tbsp olive oil

3 tbsp flour

2 cups chicken stock

1/4 cup white wine

4 tbsp lemon juice

2 tbsp lemon rind

1 lb asparagus

1–2 tbsp prepared pesto sauce

1/2 cup grated Parmesan or Asiago cheese

The White Oak Inn
29683 Walhonding Rd
Danville, OH 43014
740-599-6107
info@whiteoakinn.comwhiteoakinn
www.whiteoakinn.com

BUCKHORN INN

Marinated Beef Tenderloin

INGREDIENTS:

1 cup soy sauce

1/2 cup olive oil

3 cloves fresh garlic, chopped

1 tsp fresh thyme, or 1 tsp dried thyme

1 tsp fresh ground black pepper

1 tsp hot sauce

1 5–6 lb trimmed beef tenderloin

INSTRUCTIONS:

Combine first 6 ingredients and pour over beef. Marinate covered 4–8 hrs, turning once. Preheat charcoal broiler and pre-heat oven to 325F.

Remove beef from marinade. Brown all sides of tenderloin on broiler. Place in baking pan and bake 1½ hrs or until inserted meat thermometer reads 140F.

Bring marinade to a boil, then thicken slightly with cornstarch and water.

Slice tenderloin to desired thickness and serve with marinade.

YIELD: *10–12 large servings*
COOK TIME: *1½ hrs*

Buckhorn Inn
2140 Tudor Mtn Rd
Gatlinburg, TN 37738
865-436-4668
info@buckhorninn.com
www.buckhorninn.com

Beef Tenderloin with *Red Wine & Pistachios*

Nagle Warren Mansion
222 E 17th St
Cheyenne, WY 82001
307-637-3333
jim@nwmbb.com
www.naglewarrenmansion.com

INSTRUCTIONS:

In a large saucepan, combine the stock, red wine, shallots, 1/2 cup roasted garlic and 3/4 cup chopped parsley. Bring to a simmer over medium heat and cook until reduced (coats the back of a spoon), about 20 min.

Transfer mixture to a blender and purée until smooth. Strain through a fine sieve into another clean saucepan. Season with salt and pepper. Stir in the remaining parsley, then reduce heat to low.

In a small bowl, combine the remaining garlic, pistachios, sunflower seeds and 6 tbsp of the red wine sauce. Mix well and set aside. Rub the surface of the steaks with olive oil. Grill the steaks until well seared on the surface—both sides. Transfer to a baking dish. Bake at 300F until medium-rare.

Brush the tops of the steaks with a small amount of red wine sauce, and then press the steaks, topside down, into the pistachio mixture, coating the surface well. Position the steaks on serving platter, spoon the remaining sauce around them, garnish with parsley sprigs and serve.

YIELD: *12 servings*
COOK TIME: *45 min*

INGREDIENTS:

6 cups beef or veal stock

6 cups dry red wine, preferably Pinot Noir

1½ cups shallots, chopped

1½ cups garlic cloves, roasted

1½ cups fresh parsley, chopped

Salt and pepper to taste

3/4 cup toasted pistachios, chopped

3/4 cup sunflower seeds, chopped

12 8-oz beef tenderloin steaks

1/3 cup olive oil

Sliced Veal *in a Creamy Mushroom Sauce*

INGREDIENTS:

1 lb thinly sliced, lean veal shoulder

2 tbsp olive oil

2 cups sliced mushrooms

1 diced medium-white onion

1 cup white wine

1 cup brown gravy

1/2 cup heavy whipping cream

1 tbsp ground black pepper

1 tsp paprika powder or 1 tsp finely chopped parsley for garnish

INSTRUCTIONS:

In a large skillet, sauté thinly sliced veal in olive oil for 2 min. Add sliced mushrooms and onions and stir for 30 seconds. Remove mixture and place in bowl. Sauté white wine and gravy in same skillet for 5 min. Return veal, onions and mushrooms to skillet, add cream and cook 1 min. Add pepper and serve immediately. Garnish with parsley and paprika powder.

YIELD: *4 servings*
COOK TIME: *8–10 min*

1291 Bed & Breakfast
312 W 53rd St, Suite 6A
New York City, NY 10019
212-397-9686
1291@1291.com
www.1291.com

Excellent Marinated Roast Pork Loin

INGREDIENTS:

10 lb whole pork loin

1½ cup lite soy sauce

1½ cup apple cider

1 tbsp yellow mustard

1/4 tsp ground black pepper

1/4 tsp garlic salt

pinch onion powder

pinch dried basil

2 bay leaves

Squiers Manor

122 McKinsey Dr
Maquoketa, IA 52060
563-652-6961
innkeeper@squiersmanor.com
www.squiersmanor.com

INSTRUCTIONS:

Cut pork loin in half. With sharp knife, poke into roast at about 1-inch intervals. Pour marinade over roast slowly to cover all. Allow to stand in refrigerator 2–3 hrs (or overnight), turning roast frequently. Remove roast from marinade, reserve liquid.

Fit rack into roasting pan. Bake on rack in open pan at 450F for 15 min. Decrease heat to 325F until meat thermometer reaches 150F. Then, reduce heat to 250F and continue roasting until meat thermometer reaches 170F, about 30–45 min. Baste with reserved marinade at each temperature change. Also baste frequently with juices in pan. Finally, place lid on roasting pan or cover with foil and let rest in 200F oven until ready to serve.

YIELD: *16 servings*
COOK TIME: *2 hrs 30 min*

Duck Bombay

INGREDIENTS:

1 3-lb duckling

FOR RUB:

1 tbsp salt

1/2 tsp garlic powder

1 tsp cracked black pepper

1/2 tsp ginger powder

FOR SAUCE:

2 slices bacon

1/4 cup green onions, chopped

1/4 cup sliced almonds

1 tbsp mango chutney

1/4 cup brandy

INSTRUCTIONS:

Preheat oven to 350F. Mix dry ingredients together and rub onto duckling (there will be extra seasoning left over). Roast duckling for one hour, and let cool. Split duckling in half, if desired remove breast and leg joint bones.

Brown & julienne sliced bacon, add green onions and almonds, sauté until almonds are golden. Mix in chutney. Add brandy and mix well. Serve over duck.

YIELD: *2 servings*
COOK TIME: *1 hr*

Sunset Hill House
231 Sunset Hill Rd
Sugar Hill, NH 03586
800-786-4455
innkeeper@sunsethillhouse.com
www.sunsethillhouse.com

Cornish Hens *Baked in Champagne*

INGREDIENTS:

- 2 Cornish hens
- salt
- 1/4 cup melted butter
- freshly ground pepper
- 1/4 cup champagne
- cooked rice or pasta of your choice

INSTRUCTIONS:

Preheat oven to 425F. Clean the hens and remove the organs. Lightly salt the cavities. Brush with melted butter and lay in a baking pan, breast side up. Pepper the hens to taste. Bake for 10 min to brown. Reduce the heat to 350F, pour champagne over the hens and return to the oven for 30 to 45 min. Baste every 5 min (this seems like a lot, but it is well worth the flavor result).

Serve the hens whole or split over the bed of rice or pasta. Serves 2, or 4 if split. Also excellent served with a side of buttered brussel sprouts.

YIELD: *2–4 servings*
COOK TIME: *40–55 min*

Grandison Inn at Maney Park

1200 N Shartel Ave
Oklahoma City, OK 73103
888-799-4667
grandison@coxinet.net
www.grandisoninn.com

Crispy Braised Pork Belly

INGREDIENTS:

1 fresh pork belly

2 cups Kosher salt

2 cups granulated sugar

1/2 cup toasted, ground fall spices (cinnamon, clove, allspice, etc.)

1 large onion, diced

5 celery stalks, diced

4 carrots, peeled, diced

4 Granny Smith apples, diced

1 fennel bulb, diced

1/2 bunch fresh thyme

3 sprigs tarragon

5 bay leaves

5 star anise

10 *each* black peppercorns, allspice berries, and juniper berries

1 gallon chicken stock (or water)

2 cups apple juice

INSTRUCTIONS:

Mix salt, sugar, and spices in mixing bowl. Cover bottom of sheet pan with 1/3 of salt mixture. Lay pork belly on top and cover belly with remaining salt mixture. Cover and refrigerate 12 hrs or overnight. Wash salt mixture off belly under cold running water and pat dry.

Preheat oven to 350F. Add 1/2 of the vegetables, apples, and spices to the bottom of a braising/roasting pan. Lay belly on top and cover with remaining vegetables, apples, and spices. Bring the chicken stock/water and apple juice to a boil and pour over belly. Add enough to fully cover. Cover with foil and braise in oven for 4–6 hrs or until soft and tender. Remove and cool in liquid.

Remove belly from liquid and place on a sheet pan. Place a second sheet pan on top. Use a gallon of milk or bottles of soda to weigh it down. Refrigerate overnight.

Peel potatoes and cook gently in salted water until tender. Strain and pass through mesh strainer. Add cream and butter. Season with salt and white pepper to taste.

Julienne apples and toss with celery leaves and olive oil.

Remove belly and cut into desired size pieces. Sear, skin side down, in hot pan and place in 350F oven to cook.

Place spoonful of potato purée in center of plate. Place seared belly on top and top with apple/celery salad.

YIELD: *16 servings*
COOK TIME: *7 hrs*

POTATO PURÉE:

3 Yukon Gold Potatoes

2 cups heavy cream

1/2 cup butter

APPLE/CELERY SALAD:

1 Granny Smith apple

1 cup celery leaves, inner leaves only

L'Auberge Provencale
13630 Lord Fairfax Hwy
White Post, VA 22620
800-638-1702
celebrate@laubergeprovencale.com
www.laubergeprovencale.com

Chicken Jerusalem

INGREDIENTS:

2 boneless chicken breasts

1 tbsp butter

flour for dredging chicken

1/2 tbsp fresh chopped garlic

1 cup button mushrooms

1/2 cup quartered artichokes, frozen or canned

1/2 cup sherry

1/4 cup heavy cream

salt and pepper

Hotel Charlotte
18736 Main St
Groveland, CA 95321
209-962-6455
hotelcharlotte@aol.com
www.HotelCharlotte.com

NOTE: *With this quick and easy recipe, you will find plenty of time for a slow dance after dinner.*

INSTRUCTIONS:

Trim the chicken pieces and lightly pound to even 1/2-inch thick pieces. Cut each piece in half. Melt butter in a sauce pan. Dredge chicken in flour & sauté in butter until cooked. Add garlic, mushrooms, artichokes and sauté together for 5 min. Add sherry, heavy cream and salt and pepper to taste. Cook on high heat for approximately 5 min, until reduced by half.

YIELD: *4 servings*
COOK TIME: *15 min*

Cranberry Chicken

INSTRUCTIONS:

Lightly salt and pepper chicken breasts. Over medium heat, brown chicken in olive oil.

Mix together mustard, orange juice, and cranberry sauce in a bowl and pour over chicken. Simmer for approx. 30–45 min over moderate heat. Turn frequently to avoid burning. Once sauce thickens chicken is done. Serve with remainder of sauce over chicken. Great with brown or wild rice.

YIELD: *6 servings*
COOK TIME: *30–45 min*

INGREDIENTS:

4 deboned chicken breasts

1/2 cup Dijon mustard

1/2 cup orange juice

1 cup canned whole cranberry sauce.

Olive oil for browning

Dash of salt and pepper

***Governor's
Bed & Breakfast***

327 Union St
Milton, DE 19968
302-684-4649
wdpost@aol.com

Change Up Chicken for Two

INGREDIENTS:

2 chicken breasts

olive oil or vegetable oil

citrus (lime or lemon juice, fresh or bottled)

SEASONING:

fresh garlic, basil, oregano, cilantro, salt & pepper

OR

store-bought BBQ herb rub, hot sauce or pepper flakes, to taste (for an added kick)

NOTE: *Chicken is a key ingredient in a lighter, healthier eating style. But, who wants to eat the same dish over and over? And who wants to spend a lot of time preparing it? Here's our tasty solution:*

INSTRUCTIONS:
Measure 1½ oz of oil and add 1/2 oz citrus juice a total of 1/4 cup (should be a 3-to-1 ratio of oil to citrus juice).

For homemade seasoning, finely chop garlic (fresh or bottled) and herbs (fresh or dried); add salt and pepper to taste, and add to oil mixture.

For store-bought, add hot sauce or pepper flakes (optional) to BBQ herb rub. Add to oil mixture.

Place marinade ingredients in a Ziplock bag only large enough to hold and close around the chicken. Add chicken and allow to marinate in the refrigerator for 1/2 hr.

Light and warm up grill: Grill chicken breasts about 2 min per side (for thinly sliced, boneless/skinless breasts about 1/4-inch thick) and longer for thicker or bone-in ones (until internal temperature reaches 165F).

In the oven: Place in a roasting pan or platter with rack and grill on high for about 2 min per side (for thinly sliced, boneless/skinless breasts about 1/4-inch thick) and longer for thicker or bone-in ones (until internal temperature reaches 165F).

THE CHANGE UP:
Marinate the chicken in one of the following for a different taste each meal. There is no "right way." If you like the taste of the marinade alone you'll likely enjoy it on your chicken:
- Bottled or homemade BBQ sauce
- Bottled marinades, we recommend Asian flavors by Lawry or KC Masterpiece's Spiced Caribbean Jerk Marinade.
- Bottled or homemade Italian dressing (or olive oil and Italian-style spices)

To avoid the high fructose corn syrup found in many bottled mixes, make your own sweet marinade. Add honey or molasses. Use some oil to ensure the chicken stays moist. For something similar to the Caribbean Jerk add soy sauce, vinegar, onions and garlic (finely chopped or mashed), spices such as allspice, nutmeg, cinnamon, red pepper, dried onion and garlic.

Using a marinade with a lot of sugar will produce more grill marks due to carmelization and add more color to your meat.

Prospect Hill Inn
801 W Main St, Hwy 67
Mountain City, TN 37683
423-727-0139
judy@prospect-hill.com
www.prospect-hill.com

Chicken Pot Pie

FILLING:

1½ cups or more diced leftover chicken

1 pkg frozen mixed vegetables or 1 cup frozen peas and 1 cup frozen corn, veggies defrosted

1 potato microwaved or boiled and cubed

1 can cream of mushroom soup

1/4 tsp thyme

1 cup milk

1 tbsp plus 1/4 tsp "JIFFY" Baking Mix

1/2 tsp salt

plenty of freshly ground black pepper

TOPPING:

1½ cup "JIFFY" Baking Mix

2 eggs

3/4 cup milk

2 chopped green onions

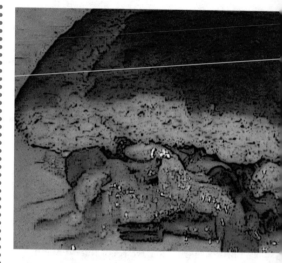

INSTRUCTIONS:
Preheat oven to 400 F.

Grease a 9x13-inch pan. Mix all filling ingredients gently and spread in dish.

Blend all topping ingredients and spoon on top of chicken mixture.

Bake 30 min until filling begins to bubble and top is lightly browned.

YIELD: *6–8 servings*
COOK TIME: *30 min*

Mango Chutney Mahi Mahi

INSTRUCTIONS:

MANGO CHUTNEY SAUCE: In blender or food processor, blend mango chutney until smooth and creamy. Place into saucepan and add remaining ingredients. Stir over low to moderate heat. Simmer for about 10 min.

Meanwhile, cut fish filet into two pieces, 1/2-inch thick. Brush both sides of fish with softened butter. Broil one side until half done. Turn fish over and broil other side. Place on serving dish and spoon 3 tsp of mango chutney sauce over the middle of each piece, sprinkle 1½ tsp chopped macadamia nuts on top of the sauce. Add a little chopped parsley.

YIELD: *2–4 servings*
COOK TIME: *10 min*

Kilauea Lodge
19-3948 Old Volcano Rd
Volcano, HI 96785
808-967-7366
stay@kilauealodge.com
www.kilauealodge.com

INGREDIENTS:

1 lb Mahi Mahi or Ahi filet

softened butter

MANGO CHUTNEY SAUCE:

2 cups mango chutney

3 oz white wine

2 oz cider vinegar

3 oz brown sugar

1 oz sherry

1 tsp white pepper

3 oz lilikoi juice (passion fruit)

2 oz pineapple juice

1 tbsp macadamia nuts, chopped

pasley for garnish

Appalachian Golden Trout

INGREDIENTS:

8 Golden Trout, cleaned

2 cups flour

16 oz stone ground cornmeal

1/2 cup buttermilk

1 cup butter

16–32 young ramps (stalks with top half of green leaf removed)

16–32 black morel mushrooms

2 Vidalia onions

2 each red, yellow and orange peppers

1 1/2 cups Durif or Petite Sirah wine

1 cup dry white wine

North Fork Mountain Inn

Smoke Hole Rd
Cabins, WV 26855
304-257-1108
nfmi@wildblue.net
www.northforkmtninn.com

INSTRUCTIONS:

Dust trout with flour. Dip in buttermilk. Gently coat with cornmeal. Melt butter (1 tbsp per fish) in sauté pan over medium heat. Cook trout until completely cooked, 3–4 min, until fish becomes flaky. Transfer fish to warmed plates.

Remove top half of green leaf from ramp stalk and discard. Finely chop ramps and sauté in 2 tbsp of butter and 1/2 cup dry white wine. Slice morel mushrooms in half and sauté in 2 tbsp butter and 1/2 cup Petite Sirah. Thinly slice Vidalia onions and sweet peppers. Sauté in 1/4 cup of butter and 1/2 cup dry white wine.

Combine ramps, mushrooms, onions and peppers and sauté on high heat for 1 min. Bring remaining cup of Petite Sirah wine to a boil and reduce to half of original volume. Evenly divide the vegetable mixture over the center of each trout filet. Drizzle 1 tbsp of the red wine reduction over each.

YIELD: *8 servings*
COOK TIME: *30 min*

Innkeeper's Mussel Chowder

INSTRUCTIONS:

Scrub mussels in cool water and remove the byssus threads or beards; discard any whose shells don't close when tapped. In an 8- to 10-quart pan, combine mussels and wine; bring to a boil over high heat. Cover and simmer over medium heat until mussels open, 5 to 8 min. Pour into a colander set in a large bowl to collect broth. Let mussels stand until cool enough to handle.

Meanwhile, peel and cut potatoes into 1/2-inch cubes. Peel and chop onion. Rinse celery and dice into 1/4-inch pieces. Wash and seed yellow/red pepper and dice.

In the pan used for mussels, melt butter over medium heat. Add onion and celery; stir often until onion is limp, 6 to 8 min. Add curry powder, cayenne pepper and basil; stir until spices become more fragrant, about 30 seconds. Pour mussel juices from bowl into pan. Add tomato sauce, cream, and potatoes.

Turn heat to high; when mixture is boiling, cover, reduce heat to low, and simmer, stirring occasionally, until flavors are well blended, about 30 min.

Meanwhile, remove mussels from shells; discard shells. Add mussels to chowder; cover and simmer just until mussels are hot, 3 to 5 min. Do not overcook. Add salt and pepper to taste. Ladle into bowls.

YIELD: *10 servings*
COOK TIME: *1 hr*

INGREDIENTS:

5 lbs mussels in shells

1 cup dry white wine

1 lb thin-skinned potatoes

1/2 lb onion (about 1 medium onion)

3 oz celery stalk (about 1 medium stalk)

1/2 yellow or red pepper

3 tbsp butter

2 tsp curry powder, mild

1/4 tsp cayenne pepper

1 1/2 tsp dried basil

1 8-oz can tomato sauce

2 cups whipping cream

salt and pepper

Shelburne Inn

4415 Pacific Way
Seaview, WA 98644
800-INN-1896
innkeeper@theshelburneinn.com
www.theshelburneinn.com

Mouthwatering Mississippi Crab Cakes

INGREDIENTS:

1 lb crab meat, lump

1/4 cup mayonnaise

1 egg, beaten

1 tbsp Creole mustard

1 tbsp lemon juice, fresh

2 tsp Old Bay Seasoning

1 tbsp cilantro, minced

1 tsp garlic, minced

2 tsp shallots, finely chopped

1 tbsp horseradish

2 tbsp yellow & red bell pepper, diced

dash of hot sauce

salt and pepper to taste

Panko bread crumbs to bind, about 1/2 cup or more

cornmeal and olive oil to brown crab cakes

INSTRUCTIONS:

Mix everything in a large stainless steel bowl, except for bread crumbs. Add the panko last. Form into 4 oz cakes, lightly dredge in cornmeal and sauté, with a little olive oil over medium heat. Brown on each side and finish in the oven at 400F for 5 min.

Serve with your favorite fresh corn salsa and aioli.

YIELD: *6 servings*
COOK TIME: *5–10 min*

Fairview Inn
734 Fairview St
Jackson, MS 39202
601-948-3429
fairview@fairviewinn.com
www.fairviewinn.com

New Orleans Style BBQ Shrimp

INGREDIENTS:

2 lbs shrimp, heads left on

1/2 lb butter

2 tbsp olive oil

2 tsp of Creole seasoning (or as an alternate, add pinch of crushed red pepper, cayenne pepper, sea salt, white pepper, and black pepper)

1 tbsp chopped, fresh garlic (adjust amount to taste)

dash of Worcestershire sauce

dash of lemon juice

4 oz beer or white wine

NOTE: *Yum, yum. Is your mouth watering yet? Serve with French or sourdough bread for dipping the sauce. Have lots of napkins or paper towels ready, as this is VERY messy. (Locals put the whole shrimp in their mouth to extract the sauce that would be wasted otherwise, before peeling the shrimp.) BBQ is a misnomer since there is **no** BBQ sauce in this recipe, but that's what they call it in N'Awlins.*

INSTRUCTIONS:
In iron skillet, sauté shrimp in butter and olive oil with seasonings, 4–5 min. Turn over when shrimp are pink. Reduce heat, add garlic and sauté 1 more min. Add Worcestershire sauce, beer or wine, and lemon juice, cover, and simmer 2–3 more min.

Dish is best when refrigerated overnight, then reheated, as it intensifies flavors.

Reheating directions: Place in preheated 400F oven for 6–8 min or until butter bubbles.

YIELD: *2 servings*
COOK TIME: *10 min*

1870 Banana Courtyard
1422 N Rampart St
New Orleans, LA 70116
(800) 842-4748
bananacour@aol.com
www.bananacourtyard.com

Shrimp Sarah

INGREDIENTS:

1/4 cup mush-rooms, sliced

3 tbsp golden raisins

2 tbsp mango ginger chutney

1/4 tsp curry powder

pinch cayenne pepper

dash Worcester-shire sauce

1/2 cup heavy cream

20 shrimp, large, shelled and deveined

3 cups wild rice, cooked

INSTRUCTIONS:

Cook the mushrooms, raisins, chutney, spices, Worcestershire sauce, and cream in a small skillet over medium heat for 5 min, or until thickened.

Arrange the shrimp on four skewers. Brush the shrimp with a little butter or oil. Broil 4 to 5 inches from heat for 4 to 5 min, turning once, or until cooked.

Serve shrimp on rice and spoon sauce over the top.

YIELD: *4 servings*
COOK TIME: *10 min*

The Peck House
83 Sunny Ave
Empire, CO 80438
303-569-9870
thepeckhouse@yahoo.com
www.thepeckhouse.com

Sambuca Shrimp

**Abingdon Manor
Inn & Restaurant**
307 Church St
Latta, SC 29565
888-752-5090
abingdon@bellsouth.net
www.abingdonmanor.com

INGREDIENTS:

1 1/2 lbs fresh shrimp

1 tsp olive oil

2 tbsp unsalted butter, divided

2 medium shallots, very finely chopped

2 tbsp dry vermouth

2 tbsp Sambuca liqueur

1/2 cup heavy whipping cream

1/2 cup peeled, seeded and chopped tomatoes

salt and freshly ground pepper to taste

12 stalks of fresh chives

INSTRUCTIONS:
Peel and de-vein shrimp. In a skillet large enough to hold the shrimp without crowding, heat olive oil and 1 tbsp butter until light brown in color. Add the shrimp and sauté for 2–3 min. Stir and turn the shrimp, then add the shallots and continue cooking, make sure not to burn them. Add the vermouth and Sambuca and let bubble until volume is reduced by half. Add the cream, tomatoes, salt and pepper. Continue to cook until sauce is thick enough to coat the bottom of a spoon.

Remove from heat and stir in remaining tbsp of butter. Pour a couple of tbsp of the finished sauce onto the bottom of a plate, arrange 4–5 shrimp in a fan and decorate with the chives.

YIELD: *6 servings*
COOK TIME: *10 min*

BLUE HERON INN

Crab Fondue

INGREDIENTS:

8 oz cream cheese

5 oz sharp cheddar cheese spread

1/4 cup half and half

1/2 tsp Worcestershire sauce

1/2 tsp garlic salt

6 oz crab meat

INSTRUCTIONS:

In a medium sauce pan mix together cheeses, half and half, Worcestershire sauce and garlic salt. Stir over low heat until melted and well blended. Add crab, breaking up large pieces.

Serve warm in a fondue pot with bread cubes.

YIELD: *4 servings*
COOK TIME: *5–7 min*

Blue Heron Inn
4175 E Menan Lorenzo Hwy
Rigby, ID 83442
208-745-9922
innkeeper@idahoblueheron.com
www.idahoblueheron.com

Tamale Pie

INSTRUCTIONS:
Preheat oven to 350F.

Grease a 6x9-inch or 8x8-inch baking dish.

Cook the ground beef in a large pan until it begins to brown. Pour off excess fat. Mix in chili powder. Add beans, salsa and green chilies. Mix in flour, salt and pepper and let simmer while you prepare topping.

Combine all topping ingredients and blend until moist, don't over-mix.

Pour meat mixture into baking dish and spoon topping over meat mixture. Bake uncovered 25 min or until lightly browned.

YIELD: *4–6 servings*
COOK TIME: *25 min*

INGREDIENTS:

1 lb ground beef

1 1/2 tsp chili powder

2 cans beans (kidney, pinquito, pinto, black, or your choice), drained

1 cup your favorite salsa (mild or hotter as your family prefers)

1 4.5-oz can green chilies

1 tbsp flour

salt and pepper

TOPPING:

1 pkg "JIFFY" Corn Muffin Mix

1/2 cup shredded cheese, cheddar or jack

1 egg

1/3 cup milk

2 chopped green onions

Sweets and Treats

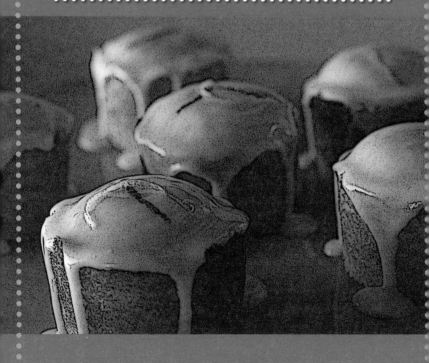

BED AND BREAKFAST INNKEEPERS understand that the best sweets and treats are created with hospitality, relaxation and tradition in mind. These morning, noon and night delicacies are an essential facet of the B&B experience and have come to be anticipated by many bed and breakfast travelers. Now that innkeepers have shared their treasured muffin, scone, cake, sweet bread, and pastry recipes with us, you can recreate these exceptional sweets and treats right at home—from their kitchen to yours!

A well-crafted dessert is not just the final touch to a fine meal; it can be the beginning of a wonderful evening. Dessert making is an art that innkeepers have taken to new heights—and you can benefit from their expertise the next time you set out to try one of these recipes. Whether you're craving pies or tortes, cobblers or crisps, blintzes or puddings, cookies or brownies, muffins or scones, tea breads or cakes, you're sure to find satisfaction for your sweet tooth. From the award-winning *Mandarin Orange Streusel Muffins* from Two Sisters Inn, to the quick and simple *Old Fashioned Fruit Cobber* (a favorite from "JIFFY"), you'll find a delectable assortment of goodies in the following pages.

Life is uncertain. Eat dessert first.

ERNESTINE ULMER

BIRD-IN-HAND VILLAGE INN & SUITES

Famous Wet-Bottomed Shoofly Pie

PIE CRUST:

2 cups all-purpose flour

1 tsp salt

3/4 cup shortening

5 tbsp water

FILLING:

1/2 cup dark corn syrup

1/4 cup light brown sugar, packed

1 large egg, beaten

1/2 tsp baking soda

1/2 cup hot water

CRUMB TOPPING:

1 cup all-purpose flour

3 tbsp shortening

2/3 cup light brown sugar, packed

pinch of salt

pinch of ground cinnamon

NOTE: *A grandma Smucker favorite, as featured in the May 2010 issue of Country Living.*

INSTRUCTIONS:
Preheat oven to 350F.

CRUST: In medium bowl, mix flour and salt. Cut shortening into flour mixture until it resembles coarse crumbs. Gradually add water until combined. Press together to form dough and chill for at least 1 hr or up to overnight. Roll out dough on lightly floured surface to 1/8 inch thickness. Fit into a 9-inch pie pan.

FILLING: Combine corn syrup, brown sugar and egg. Dissolve baking soda in hot water, stir into syrup mixture and pour into pie crust.

TOPPING: In medium bowl mix ingredients using your fingers or a pastry blender until combined. Sprinkle crumbs evenly over corn syrup mixture. Bake for 50–60 min.

YIELD: *8 servings*
COOK TIME: *50–60 min*

Bird-in-Hand Village Inn & Suites
2695 Old Philadelphia Pike
Bird in Hand, PA 17505
800-914-2473
sscharmer@bird-in-hand.com
www.bird-in-hand.com

Cheese Blintzes and *Fresh Strawberry Compote*

CRÊPES: Stir flour, sugar and salt in large bowl. Whisk eggs, milk, butter and vanilla in medium bowl to blend. Add to dry ingredients and whisk until smooth. Set aside and let sit for 20 min.

Spray pan w/ nonstick spray, heat over medium-low heat. Pour 2 tbsp crêpe batter into pan and swirl pan to coat bottom thinly. Cook until edge of crêpe is light brown, about 1 min. Carefully turn crêpe over. Cook until beginning to brown in spots, about 30 seconds. Transfer crêpe to plate w/ paper towel atop crêpe. Repeat with remaining batter, spraying pan with vegetable oil spray as needed, forming total of 16 crêpes.

FILLING: Mix cheeses in large bowl to blend. Stir in sugar, egg yolks, and vanilla extract. Place 2 tbsp filling just below center of each crêpe. Fold bottom of crêpe over filling. Fold sides in. Roll crêpe up, enclosing filling completely. Transfer blintz to plastic-lined dish.

COMPOTE: Simmer orange juice and honey in skillet over medium heat until reduced by half, about 4 min. Transfer to large bowl. Stir in vanilla extract and ground cardamom. Cover and refrigerate until chilled. Stir in strawberries.

Preheat oven to 200F. Melt 2 tbsp butter in large nonstick skillet over medium-low heat. Place 5 blintzes, seam·side down, in skillet. Cook until golden brown and crisp, about 5 minutes per side. Transfer blintzes to baking sheet; keep warm in oven. Repeat with remaining 4 tbsp butter and 11 blintzes in 2 more batches. Place blintzes on plates and cover with fresh strawberry compote. Sprinkle with powdered sugar.

YIELD: *16 servings*

INGREDIENTS:

- 1 cup flour
- 1 tbsp sugar
- pinch of salt
- 3 eggs
- 1 cup milk
- 6 tbsp butter, melted
- 1 tsp vanilla extract
- nonstick spray
- 1/2 lb ricotta cheese
- 4 oz cream cheese
- 3 tbsp sugar
- 2 egg yolks
- 1/4 tsp vanilla extract
- 1 cup orange juice
- 2/3 cup honey
- 1 tsp vanilla extract
- 1/2 tsp ground cardamom
- 4 cup strawberries
- 6 tbsp butter
- powdered sugar

Colonial Gardens B&B

1109 Jamestown Rd
Williamsburg, VA 23185
800-886-9715
innkeeper@colonial-gardens.com
www.colonial-gardens.com

Blintzes Soufflé with *Blueberry Sauce*

INGREDIENTS:

BLINTZES:

2 pkgs frozen cheese or blueberry blintzes

1/4 cup butter, melted

3 tbsp sugar

5 eggs, beaten

2 cups sour cream

1/2 tsp salt

1 tbsp vanilla extract

3 tbsp orange juice

BLUEBERRY SAUCE:

1 pint blueberries

3/4 cup of sugar

1 tbsp corn starch

dash of salt

1 tsp lemon juice

B&B at The Rock Garden

176 Brush Valley Rd
Boalsburg, PA 16827
888-620-7625
info@therockgardenbandb.com
www.therockgardenbandb.com

NOTE: *Serve with a fruit syrup, maple syrup or blueberry sauce.*

INSTRUCTIONS:

Preheat oven to 325F. Spray a 9x13-inch pan with non-stick spray. Place 12 blintzes in one layer. Whisk together the butter, sugar, eggs, sour cream, salt, vanilla, and orange juice. Pour over blintzes. Bake for 1 hr.

Prepare blueberry sauce about 30 min before serving. In a medium saucepan over medium heat, heat 1 cup water to a boil; add blueberries and return to boiling. Meanwhile, in a small bowl, combine the sugar, cornstarch and salt; stir into blueberries and cook, stirring constantly until thick. Add lemon juice.

YIELD: *12 servings*
COOK TIME: *1 hr*

Old-Fashioned Fruit Cobbler

INGREDIENTS:

4 cups fresh fruit, sliced

2 cups "JIFFY" Baking Mix

1/4 cup butter

1/2 tsp salt

1 cup milk

1 cup sugar

3/4 cup cold water

INSTRUCTIONS:
Preheat oven to 400F.

Peel and slice fruit. Spread in bottom of a 13x9-inch pan. Combine baking mix, butter and salt until crumbly. Blend in milk. Pour batter over fruit. Sprinkle sugar over batter. Pour water over sugar. Bake 30–40 min or until fruit is tender.

YIELD: *9–12 servings*
COOK TIME: *30–40 min*

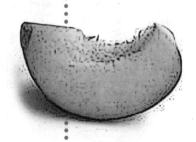

Morning Pie

INGREDIENTS:

2 cups cottage cheese

3 eggs

2/3 cup sugar

2 tbsp flour

1/3 tsp cinnamon

1/4 tsp nutmeg

2 tsp grated orange rind

1 tbsp orange juice

1/4 tsp orange extract

9" deep-dish pie shell, thawed if frozen (optional)

INSTRUCTIONS:
Preheat oven to 350F.

Beat cottage cheese with an electric mixer for 1 min. Add remaining ingredients. Blend well. Pour into pie shell or pie plate sprayed with non-stick spray and bake for 50 min, until knife inserted comes out clean.

Refrigerate overnight; serve chilled next morning. (I sometimes add cinnamon, nutmeg & more orange peel.) This pie freezes beautifully. Defrost overnight in refrigerator, slice and serve. Makes a great dessert—top with fruit and whipped cream—and a little chocolate sauce!!!

YIELD: *6 servings*
COOK TIME: *50 min*

Elk Cove Inn & Spa

6300 S Highway One
Elk, CA 95432
800-275-2967
innkeeper@elkcoveinn.com
www.elkcoveinn.com

Rhubarb Torte

INGREDIENTS:

1½ cups flour

4 tbsp powder sugar

3/4 cup butter (cut in pieces)

5 large stalks rhubarb (about 3 cups diced)

2¼ cups sugar

4 eggs

1 tbsp vanilla

1/4 tsp salt

4 tbsp flour

INSTRUCTIONS:
Heat oven to 350F.

Grease an 11x15-inch baking pan or casserole. In food processor, process flour, powdered sugar and butter until it starts to come together —approximately 1 min. Press into bottom of pan and bake for 20 min.

Dice rhubarb. Process sugar, eggs, vanilla and salt until thick. Add flour and process 10 seconds. Stir into rhubarb and spread over crust. Bake until top is brown and firm, 35 min. Cool completely before serving. Cut into squares.

YIELD: *2 dozen, depending on size*
COOK TIME: *55 min*

211 North St
Healdsburg, CA 95448
707-433-8182
info@camelliainn.com
www.camelliainn.com

Spiked Watermelon *with Fresh Mint*

INGREDIENTS:

1 8-lb watermelon, peeled, cut into 1" pieces (about 16 cups)

1 cup fresh lemon juice

2/3 cup sugar

1/2 cup vodka

6 tbsp crème de cassis

1/4 cup fresh mint

Blair House Inn
100 Spoke Hill Rd
Wimberley, TX 78676
512-847-1111
info@blairhouseinn.com
www.blairhouseinn.com

INSTRUCTIONS:

Place the watermelon in a large bowl. Whisk fresh lemon juice and sugar in a medium bowl until sugar dissolves. Whisk in the vodka and crème de cassis. Season mixture with salt to taste. Pour mixture over the watermelon. Cover and chill at least 1 hr and up to 2 hrs. Garnish with chopped mint and serve.

YIELD: *8 servings*

Biscochitos

NOTE: *These are the official state cookie of New Mexico—now there's a state with its priorities straight!*

INSTRUCTIONS:
Place dry ingredients in food processor and pulse to mix. Add the butter cut into bits and pulse until mixture resembles coarse meal. Add egg, vanilla, water, orange zest. Pulse until ball starts to form. Remove to floured surface and knead a few times. Roll dough out with rolling pin, folding over and lightly re-rolling a few times. Form into disc, wrap in film and refrigerate for at least 2 hrs.

Preheat oven to 350F. Roll out on floured surface to 1/4 inch thickness and cut into shapes with cookie cutters. Place 2 inches apart on parchment lined cookie sheets, sprinkle tops of cookies with 1/2 tsp cinnamon mixed with 2 tbsp sugar and place in freezer for 15 min. Bake for 12–14 min until slightly colored on edges but not brown.

YIELD: *2 dozen*
COOK TIME: *12–14 min*

INGREDIENTS:

2 cups flour

3/4 cups sugar

1/2 tsp baking powder

1/8 tsp salt

1 tbsp ground anise seed

12 tbsp cold butter

1 large egg

1 tsp vanilla

2 tbsp ice water

zest of 1 orange

El Rancho Merlita Ranch House B&B
1924 N. Corte El Rancho Merlita
Tucson, AZ 85715
888-218-8418
info@ranchomerlita.com
www.bedbreakfasttucsonaz.com

Orange Almond Chocolate Chippers

INGREDIENTS:

2½ cups flour

1/2 tsp baking soda

1/4 tsp salt

1 cup unsalted butter

1 cup white sugar

1/2 cup light brown sugar

2 eggs

1½ tsp natural almond extract

1½ tsp Boyajian pure orange oil or 1 tbsp grated orange rind

1½ cups Ghirardelli Double Chocolate Chips

1½ cups almonds, toasted

NOTE: *Inn at Ellis River's Featured Cookie for the Country Inns in the White Mountains Inn to Inn Cookie Tour*

INSTRUCTIONS:
Preheat oven to 350F.

Mix together flour, baking soda and salt with a wire whisk and set aside. Cream butter and sugars together well, scraping sides of bowl as needed. Add eggs, almond extract and orange oil and beat on medium speed until light and fluffy. Add flour mixture gradually, blending at low speed just until combined. Carefully mix in chocolate chips and almonds.

Drop by rounded tablespoons a full 2 inches apart onto parchment lined cookie sheet. Bake 14–16 min until cookies are slightly browned around the edges. Using a spatula, transfer cookies to a cooling rack.

YIELD: *3 dozen*
COOK TIME: *15 min*

Inn at Ellis River
17 Harriman Rd
Jackson, NH 03846
800-233-8309
stay@innatellisriver.com
www.innatellisriver.com

Breakfast Cookies to Go!

Tern Inn and Cottages
91 Chase St
West Harwich, MA 02671
800-432-3718
stay@theterninn.com
www.theterninn.com

NOTE: *Great early morning breakfast "to go." Serve with yogurt...delicious!*

INSTRUCTIONS:
Preheat oven to 350F.

Cream together butter, sugar, and vanilla. Add beaten egg, mix well.

Combine spices, baking soda, baking powder and salt with whole wheat flour, mixing gently with wire whip to blend all flavors. Add oats, dried fruits and nuts to coat with flour.

Add creamed mixture to dry ingredients and stir to combine well.

Drop dough by the spoonful on parchment lined baking sheets. Bake for 7 min, rotate sheets on rack and bake for 7 more min, until cookies are brown on edges. Cool on rack.

YIELD: *4 dozen*
COOK TIME: *14 min*

INGREDIENTS:

3/4 cup butter

1½ cups brown sugar

1 tbsp vanilla

1 egg

2 tsp cinnamon

1/4 tsp nutmeg

1/2 tsp baking soda

1/2 tsp baking powder

1/2 tsp salt

1¼ cups whole wheat flour

1⅓ cups old fashioned oats

2 cups dried fruits, cranberries, apricots, raisins, dates, apples, or any dried fruit

1 cup chopped pecans or walnuts

Chocolate Chip Cookies

INGREDIENTS:

1/2 cup butter, softened

1/2 sugar

1/2 cup brown sugar, firmly packed

1 egg

1 tsp vanilla extract

2 cups "JIFFY" Baking Mix

3/4 cup quick oats

6 oz chocolate chips

INSTRUCTIONS:
Preheat oven to 350F.

Grease a baking sheet. Cream butter, sugars, egg and vanilla. Slowly add baking mix and oats until blended. Stir in chocolate chips. Drop by tablespoon on prepared baking sheet. Bake 10–12 min or until lightly browned.

YIELD: *1½ dozen*
COOK TIME: *10–12 min*

AND ANOTHER FAVORITE FROM JIFFY...

Peanut Butter Cookies

INGREDIENTS:

1 pkg "JIFFY" Golden Yellow Mix

1 egg

3 tbsp butter, softened

1/2 cup peanut butter (smooth or crunchy)

1/2 cup mini peanut butter pieces

INSTRUCTIONS:
Preheat oven to 350F. Combine baking mix, egg, butter, and peanut butter. Stir in peanut butter pieces. Drop by tbsp on ungreased baking sheet. Press with fork in a crisscross pattern. Bake 9–12 min or until lightly browned.

YIELD: *1½ dozen*
COOK TIME: *9–12 min*

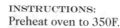

Raspberry Truffle Brownies

INSTRUCTIONS:
Preheat oven to 350F.

Coat a 9-inch round springform pan with non-stick spray. Melt unsweetened chocolate and butter in microwave-safe bowl. Add sugar, eggs and liqueur and mix well. Stir in flour and salt. Add raspberry chocolate chips and nuts if desired. Pour batter into prepared baking pan.

Bake 25–35 min and test with toothpick. There should be moist crumbs. Let cool.

When cool, run knife between brownie and pan. Remove ring. Remove bottom of pan using large knife and transfer to serving platter. Cut into 15 wedges. Garnish with powdered sugar and fresh raspberries.

YIELD: *15 servings*
COOK TIME: *25–35 min*

INGREDIENTS:

4 oz unsweetened chocolate

3/4 cup unsalted butter

2 cups granulated sugar

3 eggs

3 tbsp black raspberry liqueur

1 cup flour

1/4 tsp salt

1 cup raspberry flavored chocolate chips

1 cup chopped pecans (optional)

The Castle Inn Riverside
1155 N River Blvd
Wichita, KS 67203
316-263-9300
info@castleinnriverside.com
www.castleinnriverside.com

Brown Sugar Buttermilk Muffins

INGREDIENTS:

3 cups all-purpose flour

1½ cups brown sugar

3/4 cup cold butter

2 tsp baking powder

2 tsp ground nutmeg

1/2 tsp baking soda

1/2 tsp salt

1 cup buttermilk

2 eggs, slightly beaten

NOTE: *Muffins can be frozen. Remove from freezer 1 hr before serving. Heat in foil at 275F for 15 min.*

INSTRUCTIONS:
Preheat oven to 350F.

Mix 2 cups of the flour and brown sugar in medium bowl. Cut in butter until mixture forms coarse crumbs. Remove and reserve 3/4 cup of this mixture for topping. Add remaining 1 cup flour and remaining dry ingredients to mixture in bowl. Add buttermilk and eggs, stirring just until moistened.

Spoon batter into well greased muffin cups or paper liners in muffin cups, filling each about half-full. Sprinkle each muffin with 1½ tsp of reserved topping. Bake until wooden pick inserted in center comes out clean—about 20 min.

YIELD: *2 dozen*
COOK TIME: *20 min*

Beechwood Inn
220 Beechwood Dr
Clayton, GA 30525
706-782-5485
info@beechwoodinn.ws
www.beechwoodinn.ws

Lemon Poppy Seed Muffins

INGREDIENTS:

- 1½ cup flour
- 1 tsp baking powder
- 1/2 tsp salt
- 1/2 cup butter
- 1 cup granulated sugar
- 2 eggs
- 1/2 cup milk
- zest of one lemon
- 1/4 cup poppy seeds

INSTRUCTIONS:

In large bowl, sift together flour, baking powder and salt. In a second bowl, cream butter and sugar. Stir in eggs one at a time. Blend in milk, then lemon zest. Pour flour mixture over batter. Add poppy seeds. Stir only to moisten.

Fill greased muffin tins 3/4 full. Bake at 375F for 30–35 min.

YIELD: *1 dozen*
COOK TIME: *30–35 min*

Mount View Hotel & Spa
1457 Lincoln Ave
Calistoga, CA 94515
707-942-6877
relax@mountviewhotel.com
www.mountviewhotel.com

Cappucino Chip Muffins

INGREDIENTS:

MUFFINS:

2 cups flour

3/4 cup sugar

2 1/2 tsp baking powder

2 tsp instant espresso powder

1/2 tsp salt

1/2 tsp ground cinnamon

1 cup milk

1/2 cup butter

1 egg, lightly beaten

1 tsp vanilla extract

3/4 cup mini chocolate chips

SPREAD:

4 oz cream cheese, softened

1 oz semi-sweet chocolate

1 tbsp sugar

1/2 tsp vanilla

1/2 tsp instant espresso powder

INSTRUCTIONS:

MUFFINS:
Preheat oven to 375F.

Melt butter and heat milk to scalding. Allow both to cool. Sift together flour, sugar, baking powder, espresso coffee powder, salt, and cinnamon. In another bowl, stir together milk, butter, egg, and vanilla until blended. Make a well in center of dry ingredients, add milk mixture and stir just to combine. Stir in chips. Spoon batter into greased muffin tins. Bake at 375F for 15–20 min or until top springs back when touched. Turn out muffins onto wire rack.

SPREAD:
Melt chocolate and allow to cool. Place cream cheese, chocolate, sugar, vanilla, and espresso powder in a small bowl and blend thoroughly until smooth and of a consistent color. To serve, allow 10 min to soften at room temperature. Serve muffins with a generous amount of Chocolate Espresso Cream Cheese Spread.

YIELD: *1 dozen*
COOK TIME: *15–20 min*

7 Gables Inn & Suites

4312 Birch Ln
Fairbanks, AK 99708
907-479-0751
gables7@alaska.net
www.7gablesinn.com

Maine Blueberry Muffins

Brunswick Inn

165 Park Row
Brunswick, ME 04011
800-299-4914
info@thebrunswickinn.com
www.brunswickin-
nparkrow.com

INGREDIENTS:

1 cup milk

1/4 cup oil

1 egg

2 cups flour

1/4 cup sugar

3 tsp baking powder

1/2 tsp salt

1 cup blueberries

cinnamon sugar to taste (1 part cinnamon, 10 parts sugar)

INSTRUCTIONS:
Pre-heat oven to 400F.

Combine the milk, oil and egg. In a separate bowl, sift together flour, sugar, baking powder, and salt. Add blueberries so they are mixed well into the flour mixture. Stir in the liquid ingredients until just moistened.

Spoon the batter into well greased muffin cups; sprinkle with cinnamon sugar mixture on top. Bake approximately 20 min. Check after 15 min to avoid overcooking.

YIELD: *1 dozen*
COOK TIME: *20 min*

Orange Muffins

INGREDIENTS:

3/4 cup cooking oil

1 cup sugar

2 eggs

1½ cups flour

1 tsp salt

1 tsp baking soda

1 tsp vanilla

1/4 cup fresh orange juice

2 tbsp grated orange rind

INSTRUCTIONS:

Preheat oven to 350F.

Combine oil, sugar and eggs. Mix well. Add remaining ingredients. Blend. Pour into muffin pan sprayed with nonstick spray. Bake for 14 to 17 min.

OPTIONAL: Glaze muffins with 1/2 cup powdered sugar mixed with about a tbsp of orange juice.

YIELD: *1 dozen*
COOK TIME: *14–17 min*

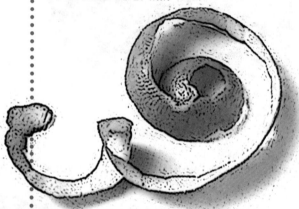

Rosevine Inn
415 S Vine
Tyler, TX 75702
903-592-2221
rosevine@dctexas.net
www.rosevine.com

Black Bear Inn Muffins

NOTE: *Add flavor by stirring citrus zest into sour cream. Use classic combinations like orange zest with dried cranberries or lemon zest with blueberries. Consider sprinkling granulated sugar on top of muffins before baking for a sweeter finish.*

INSTRUCTIONS:
Preheat oven to 350F.

Sift together flour, baking powder, salt, cinnamon, and nutmeg. In another bowl, mix milk, butter, sour cream or yogurt, eggs, vanilla and sugar. Fold wet mixture into dry ingredients. This forms the basic batter.

Now, stir in nuts and/or fruit. When using dried fruit, add an additional tbsp sour cream to the batter.

Deposit batter into mini muffin pan to which non-stick spray has been applied generously. Bake for 20–25 min.

YIELD: *2 dozen*
COOK TIME:
20–25 min

INGREDIENTS:

1 1/4 cups all purpose flour

1 1/4 tsp baking powder

1/2 tsp salt

2 tsp cinnamon

1/2 tsp nutmeg

1/4 cup milk

1/8 cup melted butter

1/2 cup sour cream or plain yogurt

2 eggs

2 tsp vanilla extract

1/2 cup sugar

1/3 cup nuts and/or fruit

Black Bear Inn
4010 Bolton Access Rd
Bolton Valley, VT 05477
800-395-6335
blkbear@wcvt.com
www.blackbearinn.travel

Mandarin Orange Streusel Muffins

INGREDIENTS:

STREUSEL TOPPING:

1/4 cup flour

1/2 cup granulated sugar

pinch salt

3 tbsp cold butter

MUFFINS:

2 eggs, slightly beaten

1/2 cup *each* brown sugar, packed, and vegetable oil

8 oz low-fat sour cream

11 oz can Mandarin orange segments, 1/4 cup reserved liquid

1 tbsp orange extract

1 tsp vanilla extract

1/4 cup orange-peach-mango juice

2 cups flour

2 tsp baking powder

1/2 tsp *each* baking soda and salt

1/2 cup chopped pecans, toasted

INSTRUCTIONS:

Prepare streusel topping by combining flour, granulated sugar and salt in a small bowl. Cut butter into mixture with pastry blender until mixture is crumbly. Set aside.

In a separate large bowl, combine beaten eggs and brown sugar. Add oil and sour cream. Drain orange segments, then dice, reserving liquid. Add diced oranges, orange and vanilla extracts, juice, and 1/4 cup reserved orange liquid.

Sift in dry ingredients and stir just until moistened. Fold in pecans. Fill greased and floured muffin pans 2/3 full. Spoon Streusel topping equally over the muffins.

Bake in a 400F oven for 18–20 min or until toothpick inserted in center comes out clean. Cool before serving.

YIELD: *1 dozen*
COOK TIME: *18–20 min*

Two Sisters Inn
10 Otoe Place
Manitou Springs, CO 80829
719-685-9684
info@twosisinn.com
www.twosisinn.com

Blueberry Corn Muffins

INGREDIENTS:

1$\frac{1}{2}$ cups all-purpose flour

1/2 cup whole wheat flour

1/2 cup cornmeal

1/2 cup sugar

2$\frac{1}{2}$ tsps baking powder

1/2 tsp baking soda

1/2 tsp salt

1/2 cup buttermilk

1/2 cup orange juice

1/2 cup butter melted

1 egg beaten

1 tbsp grated orange zest

2 cups fresh blueberries (1 pt)

INSTRUCTIONS:

Preheat oven to 400F.

In a large bowl, combine flours, cornmeal, sugar, baking powder, baking soda, and salt. In a small bowl, combine the buttermilk, orange juice, butter, egg, and orange zest. Add wet mixture to the flour mixture and blend just until the dry ingredients are moistened. Fold in blueberries.

Scoop the batter into the prepared muffin cups and bake for 15–20 min or until a wooden toothpick inserted in the center comes out clean. Turn out on a wire rack to cool.

YIELD: *1 dozen*
COOK TIME: *15–20 min*

Fairthorne B&B

111–115 Ocean St
Cape May, NJ 08204
800-438-8742
fairthornebnb@aol.com
www.fairthorne.com

Decadent Peanut Butter Bars

INGREDIENTS

1 box (1 lb) confectioner's sugar

1 cup (8 oz) graham cracker crumbs

1/8 tsp salt (optional)

1 cup (2 sticks) margarine

1 cup (8 oz) peanut butter

2 cups chocolate chips

A B&B at Dartmouth House

215 Dartmouth St
Rochester, NY 14607
800-724-6298
stay@dartmouthhouse.com
www.dartmouthhouse.com

NOTES: *No baking! Plus simple ingredients! Simply delicious! These are so easy and so good that you just might make them every week! Served with a piping hot cup of tea or coffee—any time—they're to die for!*

INSTRUCTIONS:

Mix the confectioner's sugar, graham cracker crumbs, and salt together in one bowl. In a second bowl, melt the margarine and mix in the peanut butter. Combine ingredients together and mix well, first with a spoon and then with your hands. Pat mixture into a foil-lined, ungreased 13x9-inch pan. Melt the chocolate chips and spread over the mixture.

Cool in the refrigerator for about 30 min. Remove and score the chocolate into pieces before chocolate hardens. Return to the refrigerator. Cut all the way through pieces before serving.

These can be eaten in less than 1 hr after putting in the refrigerator. Store covered in the refrigerator or you can freeze them and keep frozen for up to 3 months.

YIELD: *40–60 small bars*

Cowboy Scones

INSTRUCTIONS:

To toast coconut, preheat oven to 350F. Spread 1/2 cup flaked, sweetened coconut on baking sheet and toast in oven for 5 to 7 min until just beginning to turn golden brown. Cool before using on scones.

Preheat oven to 375F.

Put all dry ingredients in medium bowl. Add butter to mixture and cut in with pastry blender. Mix together the wet ingredients and add them to the flour mixture. Add chocolate chips, coconut, cranberries, pecans, and raisins and mix in well. This makes a sticky, shaggy dough. Knead dough on a lightly floured surface for about 12 turns (1 to 2 min) or until all ingredients are thoroughly combined. Use a mini-scone pan (16 small scones). Spray the scone pan with butter-flavored cooking spray. Fill with scone batter. Bake for 18 to 25 min. Cool. When cool, glaze with cream cheese/confectioner's sugar glaze and top with toasted coconut. Let dry and serve.

YIELD: *16 mini-scones*
COOK TIME: *18–25 min*

B Street House B&B
58 N. B St
Virginia City, NV 89440
775-847-7231
innkeepers@bstreethouse.com
www.bstreethouse.com

INGREDIENTS:

1¾ cups flour

2 tsp baking powder

1/2 tsp baking soda

1/4 tsp salt

1/4 cup brown sugar

1 tbsp granulated sugar

1 tsp ground cinnamon

1 stick cold butter

1 cup buttermilk

1 tsp vanilla extract

1 large egg

1/3 cup *each*: semi-sweet chocolate chips; white chocolate chips; coconut, flaked and sweetened; dried cranberries; pecans, finely chopped; dark raisins

CREAM CHEESE GLAZE:

4 oz cream cheese, softened

2 cups confectioners sugar

2 to 3 tbsp cream or half and half

Mayhurst Inn Sugar Scones

INGREDIENTS:

2 cups flour

1/2 cup sugar

4 tsp baking powder

3/4 tsp salt

1/2 cup cold butter

2 eggs, beaten

1/4 cup milk, half and half, or cream

1/2 cup interior garnish (raisins, chopped almonds, chocolate chips, cinnamon chips, chopped dried fruit, etc.)

NOTE: *Can be frozen and reheated briefly, but never as good as fresh.*

INSTRUCTIONS:
Preheat oven to 375F.

Mix flour, sugar, baking powder and salt together. Cut in butter with pastry cutter or 2 knives. Mix eggs with milk and add to dry ingredients. Do not over mix. Add interior garnish. Drop by spoonfuls onto ungreased or parchment lined sheet pan. Bake 14 to 15 min.

Brush tops with butter and sprinkle with coarse sugar.

YIELD: *16 servings*
COOK TIME: *14–15 min*

Mayhurst Inn
12460 Mayhurst Ln
Orange, VA 22960
888-672-5597
mayhurstbandb@aol.com
www.mayhurstinn.com

Harry's White Chocolate Apricot Scones

INGREDIENTS:

- 4 cups flour
- 2/3 cup sugar
- 2 tbsp baking powder
- 1/4 cup butter, cold
- 1 cup walnuts, chopped
- 1 cup dried apricots, diced
- 1 cup white chocolate chips
- 2 eggs
- 1 cup heavy cream
- 2 tsp vanilla

INSTRUCTIONS:

In a large bowl, combine nuts, diced apricots (hint: if too sticky; put in freezer for awhile—they'll be easier to dice) and white chocolate chips.

Process flour, sugar, baking powder and butter in food processor until it looks crumbly. If you don't have food processor, cut cold butter into dry ingredients with a pastry blender. Pour into fruit/nut mixture.

In a separate bowl, combine eggs, cream and vanilla. Pour the liquid into the dry ingredients. Mix together with hands until barely combined.

Pat dough into two 8-inch circles, about 1-inch thick. Cut each into 10 triangular wedges. Brush tops with a little heavy cream. Arrange on cookie sheet.

Bake at 350F for about 18–20 min.

YIELD: *20 servings*
COOK TIME: *18–20 min*

Moondance Inn
1105 W 4th St
Red Wing, MN 55066
651-388-8145
info@moondanceinn.com
www.moondanceinn.com

Oat and Fruit Scones

INGREDIENTS:

2 cups "JIFFY" Baking Mix

3/4 cups sugar

1/2 cup oats

1/3 cup butter

1 cup dried fruit

1/2 cup milk

1 egg

INSTRUCTIONS:
Preheat oven to 400F.

Mix together the baking mix, sugar and oats. Cut in the butter. Add dried fruit and stir. In a second bowl, beat an egg with the milk and add to the mix.

Place dough on a greased baking sheet in an 8-inch circle. Let sit for about 5 min. Score dough with a knife as though you are cutting a pie.

Sprinkle with a tbsp of sugar and cook for 17–20 min at 400F.

YIELD: *1 dozen*
COOK TIME: *17–20 min*

Chocolate Chip *Pumpkin Bread*

INSTRUCTIONS:
Preheat oven to 350F.

Grease and flour loaf pan. In a medium bowl, stir together all of the dry ingredients, except the sugar. In a mixing bowl, cream together the butter and sugar. Beat in pumpkin, eggs and water. Blend pumpkin mixture in dry ingredients on low speed until just incorporated.

Pour into loaf pan and bake for approximately 1 hr. Cool in pan for 10 min and then turn out onto a cooling rack.

YIELD: *1 loaf*
COOK TIME: *1 hr*

INGREDIENTS:

1¼ cups whole wheat flour

1/4 cup cornmeal

1 tsp baking soda

1/2 tsp *each* ground ginger and cinnamon

1/4 tsp *each* ground cloves, nutmeg, and salt

1/2 cup chocolate chips

1/4 cup chopped walnuts

6 tbsp butter, soft

1 cup sugar

1 cup canned organic pumpkin (add 1/4 cup water if you are using non-organic pumpkin)

2 eggs

Solomons Victorian Inn
125 Charles St
Solomons, MD 20688
410-326-4811
info@solomonsvictorianinn.com
www.solomonsvictorianinn.com

KALTENBACH'S

Pumpkin Roll

INGREDIENTS:
BATTER:

3 eggs

1 cup sugar

3/4 cup flour

1 tsp cinnamon

1 tsp baking soda

2/3 cup cooked
pumpkin

FILLING:

8 oz cream cheese,
softened

1/4 cup butter,
softened

1 tsp vanilla

1 cup powdered
sugar

Kaltenbach's
743 Stonyfork Rd
Wellsboro, PA 16901
570-724-4954
www.kaltenbachsinn.com

INSTRUCTIONS:

Mix eggs and sugar together. Add flour, cinnamon, baking soda and pumpkin. Spread into cookie sheet lined with wax paper (grease pan and put wax paper on top, then grease and flour wax paper).

Bake at 350F for 15 min. Do not overbake. Remove warm cake from pan onto a dish towel covered with powdered sugar. Wrap up in towel and let cool.

Using cream cheese and butter of the same softness, blend cream cheese, butter, vanilla and powdered sugar. Unwrap cake and spread with filling. Roll up like a jellyroll and wrap in aluminum foil. Keep refrigerated. Slice and serve.

YIELD: *1 loaf*
COOK TIME: *15 min*

Caramel Apple Dip

INGREDIENTS:

8 tbsp butter

1 cup dark brown sugar

4 tsp vanilla

1 cup sour cream

sliced Granny Smith apples

NOTE: *Best served with tart apple slices— Granny Smiths or Empires.*

INSTRUCTIONS:
On stovetop, melt butter on medium-low heat. Add brown sugar and stir to dissolve. Add vanilla, remove from heat. Briskly stir in sour cream until blended well. Serve warm, or chill for 2 hrs to thicken.

YIELD: *6 cups*
COOK TIME: *10 min*

Inn at the Park B&B
233 Dyckman Ave
South Haven, MI 49090
269-639-1776
info@innpark.com
www.innpark.com

Chocolate Applesauce Cake

INGREDIENTS:

1½ cups shortening

6 eggs

4 cups sugar

6 cups sifted flour

1½ tsp cinnamon

6 tbsp cocoa

4½ tsp baking soda

1½ tsp salt

44 oz applesauce

4 tbsp sugar

1 cup of chopped walnuts

Shady Oaks Country Inn

399 Zinfandel Ln

St. Helena, CA 94574

707-963-1190

shdyoaks@napanet.net

www.shadyoakscoun-tryinn.com

INSTRUCTIONS:

Preheat oven 350F.

In a large mixer or food processor, cream together shortening, eggs, and 4 cups of sugar. Add flour, cinnamon, cocoa, baking soda, salt, and applesauce, and mix. Mix together 4 tbsp sugar with chopped walnuts and sprinkle on bottom of 2 floured bundt pans. Divide the batter evenly into the 2 bundt pans. Bake for approximately 1 hr or until cake test comes out clean.

YIELD: *2 cakes*
COOK TIME: *1 hr*

Ultra Lemon Tea Cake

INSTRUCTIONS:
Preheat oven to 350F.

Grease 8-inch square pan generously and dust with flour.

Blend cake mix, egg, water, lemon extract and grated lemon peel for 30 seconds. Beat for 3–4 min at medium speed. (Hand mix, beat 300 strokes.)

Bake for 20–25 min. Cake is done if it springs back when pressed lightly in center.

While cake is baking, in a small sauce pan, reduce the juice of the lemon with an equal amount of sugar and add water. Simmer on low heat until reduced by half. Once the cake is removed from oven, gently prick deeply with a fork. Let cake cool for 10 min, then remove from pan, place on plate and slowly pour lemon syrup all over the cake. Let cool completely before serving. Serve sliced by itself, or top with berries and a dollop of whipped cream.

YIELD: *4–6 servings*
COOK TIME: *20–25 min*

INGREDIENTS:

1 pkg "JIFFY" Golden Yellow Cake Mix

1 egg

1/2 cup cold water

2 tsp lemon extract

1 lemon's finely grated peel

LEMON SYRUP:

juice of 1/2 lemon

1 tbsp water

2–3 tbsp sugar

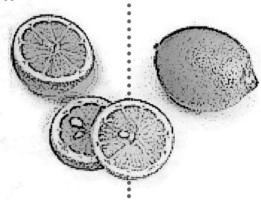

Chocolate Bits Cake

INGREDIENTS:

1 cup butter

1/2 cup sugar

1/2 cup brown sugar

3-4 ripe mashed bananas

1 cup sour cream or plain yogurt

2 tsp baking soda

2 tsp baking powder

1 tsp cinnamon

3 cups flour

2 cups chocolate chips

1 cup chopped nuts

NOTE: *"Chocolate Bits Cake" was the standard birthday and special occasion cake that my German mother-in-law made. It was a favorite of all and was very good, but over the years we added more chocolate chips and some bananas. Don't tell, but now we like it even more.*

INSTRUCTIONS:
Preheat oven to 325F.

Cream butter and sugar. Mix in brown sugar, bananas, sour cream (or yogurt), baking soda, baking powder, and cinnamon. Fold in flour, add chocolate chips and nuts and stir until just mixed.

Bake in a tube pan for approximately 1 hr or until toothpick comes out clean. Cool & sprinkle with confectioners sugar just before serving.

YIELD: *12 servings*
COOK TIME: *1 hr*

803 Elizabeth B&B
803 Elizabeth Ln
Matthews, NC 28105
704-841-8900
martha@803elizabeth.com
www.803elizabeth.com

Tropical Pumpkin Bread

INGREDIENTS:

2 cups sugar

5 eggs

1½ cups oil

2 cups canned pumpkin

3 cups flour

2 tsp soda

1 tsp cinnamon

1 tsp salt

2 pkgs instant coconut pudding mix

1 cup chopped nuts, any kind

INSTRUCTIONS:
Preheat oven to 350F.

In a medium bowl, mix together first four ingredients. Stir in flour, soda, cinnamon and salt. Blend in pudding mix and stir in nuts. Pour into 2 loaf pans.

Bake in 350F oven for 45 min or until toothpick inserted in center comes out clean.

YIELD: *2 loaves*
COOK TIME: *45 min*

Magnolia Plantation
309 SE 7th St
Gainesville, FL 32601
352-375-6653
info@magnoliabnb.com
www.magnoliabnb.com

Apricot Croissant Bread Pudding

INGREDIENTS:

1 cup Grand Marnier or other orange liqueur

1/4 cup water

5 cups whipping cream

6 large eggs

1 cup sugar

1 tbsp vanilla extract

1/2 tsp grated nutmeg

8 croissants, cubed (about 1 lb)

1 cup dried apricots, diced

caramel sauce

The Winchester Inn, Restaurant & Wine Bar

35 S Second St

Ashland, OR 97520

800-972-4991

innkeeper@thewinchesterinn.com

www.winchesterinn.com

INSTRUCTIONS:

Simmer Grand Marnier and 1/4 cup water in heavy medium saucepan for 5 min. Cool mixture completely. Whisk Grand Marnier-water mixture, cream, eggs, sugar, vanilla and nutmeg in large bowl to blend. Place croissant pieces in 13x9x2-inch glass baking dish; add apricots and toss to combine. Pour custard over croissant-apricot mixture, pressing down gently with rubber spatula so that croissant and apricot pieces are evenly covered. Let stand 20 min.

Preheat oven to 350F. Cover baking dish with aluminum foil. Place dish in larger roasting pan. Add enough hot water to roasting pan to come 1 inch up sides of baking dish. Bake 1 hr. Remove aluminum foil and continue baking until bread pudding is golden brown on top and firm to touch, about 30 min longer. Carefully remove bread pudding from oven and from water bath; cool slightly. Drizzle bread pudding with caramel sauce, if desired, and serve warm.

YIELD: *12 servings*
COOK TIME: *1 hr 30 min*

Chocolate Tea Bread

INSTRUCTIONS:
Preheat oven to 350F.

In a large bowl, sift together flour, cocoa, baking soda, salt, baking powder. Cream butter and sugar with electric mixer. Blend in eggs. Add applesauce and water alternately with dry ingredients. Stir together. Stir in chocolate pieces and nuts.

Pour into greased and floured loaf pan. Bake at 350F for 1 hr until toothpick comes out clean. Cool in pan for five min before turning out onto a wire rack. Slice and serve warm.

YIELD: *6 servings*
COOK TIME: *1 hr*

INGREDIENTS:

1 1/2 cups flour

1/3 cup cocoa

1 tsp baking soda

3/4 tsp salt

1/4 tsp baking powder

1/3 cup butter

1 1/3 cups sugar

2 eggs

1/2 cup applesauce

1/3 cup water

1/3 cup semi-sweet chocolate chips

1/3 cup chopped nuts

Arbor House, An Environmental Inn
3402 Monroe St
Madison, WI 53711
608-238-2981
arborhouse@tds.net
www.arbor-house.com

JIFFY

Great Plains Coffee Cake *– A North Dakota Favorite*

CAKE:

1½ cups "JIFFY" Baking Mix

1/2 cup sugar

3 tbsp vanilla instant pudding

1/2 cup milk

2 tbsp sour cream

1/2 cup softened butter

1/2 tsp vanilla

1/2 tsp cinnamon

1 egg

TOPPING:

1/4 cup "JIFFY" Baking Mix

1/2 cup brown sugar

1 tsp cinnamon

1/4 cup butter

1/2 cup chopped nuts

1/2 cup oats

NOTE: *This is one of Pamela Lanier's favorite afternoon treats. Her Aunt Carrie, orignally from Hungary, settled in North Dakota and brought this marvelous coffee cake recipe with her. Pamela slightly adapted the recipe and made it more time-friendly by using "JIFFY" Baking Mix (you can find the original recipe, Aunt Carrie's Hungarian Coffee Cake, in the online recipe collection on LanierBB.com).*

INSTRUCTIONS:
Preheat oven to 350F.

Spray a 9-inch round cake pan. In a bowl, beat all ingredients with a large fork 30 strokes, or with an electric mixer on low speed for 30 seconds. Continue to beat until you have a smooth texture. Pour into the prepared pan. Combine topping ingredients and sprinkle over batter. Bake for 40–45 min.

YIELD: *9 servings*
COOK TIME: *40–45 min*

Rhubarb Ripple Coffee Cake

RHUBARB PURÉE: Place the rhubarb in a 1$\frac{1}{2}$-quart, heavy-bottomed saucepan. Toss with sugar and cornstarch. Cook on low heat, covered, for about 5 min. Remove the cover, and cook on medium-low heat to cook down the fruit, stirring occasionally, about 10 to 15 min, until the fruit is very soft, and the sauce is smooth and thickened. Let cool completely.

Preheat oven to 350F. Spray a 9-inch removable-bottom tart or quiche pan or 9-inch springform pan with vegetable oil spray. In a large bowl, combine the flour and sugar. Using a mixer, your hands, a fork or a pastry blender, cut in the butter until the mixture is crumbly and mealy. Set aside 1/2 cup for topping.

To the remaining flour/sugar mixture, add the baking powder, baking soda, cinnamon, orange zest or oil, and salt. Stir in the egg, vanilla extract and buttermilk or sour milk. Spread 2/3 of the batter over the bottom and up the sides of the prepared pan. Spread the rhubarb on top of the batter, and spoon or dollop the remaining batter over the rhubarb. Sprinkle with the reserved sugar/flour mixture. Bake the cake for 40–45 min, or until the top crust is golden brown around the edges, and slightly brown in the center. Cool thoroughly. Dust with confectioners sugar just before serving.

YIELD: *12 servings*
COOK TIME: *40–45 min*

Grape Arbor Bed and Breakfast

51 E Main St, North East PA 16428
866-725-0048
grapearborbandb@aol.com | www.grapearborbandb.com

BASIC RHUBARB PURÉE:

3$\frac{1}{2}$ cups rhubarb, cut in 1" dice

3/4 cup granulated sugar

3$\frac{1}{2}$ tbsp cornstarch

COFFEE CAKE:

1$\frac{1}{3}$ cups rhubarb purée or sauce

2$\frac{1}{4}$ cups flour

3/4 cup granulated sugar

3/4 cup (1$\frac{1}{2}$ sticks) unsalted butter

1 tsp baking powder

1/2 tsp baking soda

1/2 tsp cinnamon

1 tbsp orange zest, finely minced, or 1/4 tsp orange oil

a heaping 1/4 tsp salt

1 egg, beaten

1 tsp vanilla extract

3/4 cup buttermilk

confectioners sugar for dusting

Organic Sour Cream Coffee Cake

INGREDIENTS:

STREUSEL:

2 tbsp organic flour

2 tbsp butter

5 tbsp sugar

1/2 tsp cinnamon

1 tsp cardamom

1/4 tsp fresh grated nutmeg

CAKE:

1 1/2 cups organic flour

1 cup turbinado organic sugar

2 tsp baking powder

1/2 tsp baking soda

1/4 tsp sea salt

1 cup organic sour cream or yogurt

2 organic local eggs

1 tsp organic vanilla

2 tsp lemon or lime juice

sliced local apples or any seasonal local fruit

INSTRUCTIONS:

Preheat oven to 350F.

Make the streusel first while other ingredients come to room temperature, blending the 2 tbsp flour, butter, 5 tbsp sugar, cinnamon, cardamom, and nutmeg, until crumbled.

Sift before measuring the 1 1/2 cups organic flour. Resift with turbinado sugar, baking powder, baking soda, and sea salt.

Combine and beat well: yogurt or sour cream, eggs, vanilla, and lime or lemon juice.

Add sifted ingredients to the cream mixture. Beat until smooth. Spread in 9x9-inch lightly greased pan. Sprinkle streusel with chopped nuts and apple slices that are drizzled w/ a bit of lime juice. Gently run knife thru streusel batter. Bake for approximately 20 min until knife sticks in and comes out clean.

YIELD: *10 servings*
COOK TIME: *20 min*

Montfair Resort Farm
5212 Walnut Level Rd
Crozet, VA 22932
434-823-5202
montfair@ntelos.net
www.montfairresortfarm.com

Best Ever Apple Crisp

INSTRUCTIONS:
Preheat oven to 350F.

In food processor, blend sugar, butter and flour. Add cinnamon, oats and walnuts and pulse until mixture forms very coarse crumbs. Peel and slice apples. Arrange in buttered baking dish. Top with crumb mixture and bake for 1 hr.

YIELD: *8 servings*
COOK TIME: *1 hr*

INGREDIENTS:

1 cup sugar

1/2 cup unsalted cold butter

3/4 cup whole wheat flour

1 tsp cinnamon

1/2 cup rolled oats

1/2 cup walnuts, chopped

6–8 Granny Smith apples

Isaiah Jones Homestead
165 Main St
Sandwich, MA 02563
(800) 526-1625
info@isaiahjones.com
www.isaiahjones.com

INNS AND B&BS BY STATE

Index

Food is

our common

ground,

a universal

experience.

JAMES BEARD